Don't Dump the Dog

Don't Dump the Dog

Outrageous Stories and Simple Solutions to Your Worst Dog Behavior Problems

RANDY GRIM with **MELINDA ROTH**

foreword by **LORETTA SWIT**

SKYHORSE PUBLISHING

Skyhorse Publishing books may be purchased in bulk at special discounts for sales promotion, corporate gifts, fund-raising, or educational purposes. Special editions can also be created to specifications. For details, contact the Special Sales Department, Skyhorse Publishing, 555 Eighth Avenue, Suite 903, New York, NY 10018 or info@skyhorsepublishing.com.

www.skyhorsepublishing.com

Photographs by Donna Lochmann

10 9 8 7 6 5 4 3

Library of Congress Cataloging-in-Publication Data

Grim, Randy.
Don't dump the dog : outrageous stories and simple solutions to your worst dog behavior problems / Randy Grim with Melinda Roth ; foreword by Loretta Swit.
      p. cm.
ISBN 978-1-60239-640-1 (pbk. : alk. paper)
1. Dogs--Behavior--Anecdotes. 2. Dogs--Behavior--Miscellanea. I. Roth, Melinda. II. Title.
 SF433.G75 2009
 636.7'0887--dc22
                              2009014216

Printed in the United States of America

In memory of Charley, Bear, and Stinky.
Dad misses you!

Contents

Foreword

To write what amounts to a textbook, a how-to book, and turn learning "how to" into a great read while being knee-slapping hilarious—this is a gift. This is extraordinary.

Reading *Don't Dump the Dog*, I found myself laughing out loud while learning some very valuable lessons in canine behavior. What could be better? The best way to teach is with humor. The best way to learn is through laughter. Randy is enlightened, often profound, always touching, and surely inspired.

My eyes were slamming shut with laughter and at the same time, there I was, absorbing valuable advice for training my terrier—the word, "terrier," by the way, is, I am convinced, derivative of the word "terrorist." I trust I've made my point.

While knee-slapping and jack-knifing myself into a state just short of a nosebleed, I was learning how to keep her barking down to a meaningful minimum (she is allowed to bark at burglars) and how to housebreak without actually breaking the house or the furniture therein.

Randy's written a book with intelligence, fired by his passion and compassion, drawing on expertise from years of hands-on experience, and flavored it with wit as sharp as his pen. He continues to prove that the power of one is a powerful force indeed. His passion continues to ignite that of his friends, his volunteers, and colleagues.

He continues to reinforce our strength to persevere in the rescue and protection of these helpless, abandoned, often-abused animals who depend on us for their survival.

It's serious, yes. It's grave. Yet he manages to keep us aloft with his self-deprecating humor and his relentless spirit.

He reflects on his home collection of strays so damaged they cannot be placed elsewhere; Charley, for example, he notes, needs to wear a basket muzzle which makes him resemble Hannibal Lecter, at which point I fell off my chair laughing, serious pains in my ribcage. I was in imminent danger of having tears roll down not only my cheek, but my leg as well when I read that he yearned to bring Charley for a meaningful visit to Michael Vick's, volunteering to bring the Chianti and fava beans. At this point, I fell forward onto my computer where I nearly concussed myself.

To all of us working in the humane environment, and to the many new fans and friends he will seduce with this book, Randy is an inspiration. An amazing man who is part canine, part whisperer/therapist, part saint, and part clown; a five-star general leading his troops in a massive rescue mission in a battle against cruelty. His compassion is boundless, his humor infectious, his spirit indefatigable.

There are few vocations as painful and heart-wrenching as rescue work. Yet, bereft of sermons and preaching, his message reaches into your heart by way of your funny bone—and stays there.

Loretta Swit

Los Angeles, 2009

Acknowledgments

I would like to thank my buddy, Melinda, for thinking I am funny, and my mom, Mary Ellen, for putting up with me and my clan. Thanks to my wonderful Stray Rescue family, and to Jenn Foster and Darrell Antalick for their friendship. Thanks also to Jill-Michele Melean and to my editor Ann Treistman and my agent Julie Castiglia, for believing in this book. I would also like to thank Dr. A for listening to my rants and for my Paxil so I could write this book.

Don't Dump the Dog

Introduction

I arrive at my therapist's office with an e-mail clutched in my fist. This time, I think, I'll *show* him what I deal with every day, and then maybe he'll finally understand.

I toss the crumpled e-mail onto his desk.

"What is this?"

"Just read it," I say, assuming my usual position on the couch. "Out loud."

For the record, Dr. Gupta is my fourth therapist since I founded Stray Rescue fifteen years ago, and during all of those years—through the book tours, the television shows, the movie deals, the awards—he's come closer than any of them to understanding my "issues." I can tell that he still considers me crazy, though, so it's important that I appear calm and rational.

As Dr. Gupta unfolds and flattens out the e-mail, I stare up at the ceiling. I know it well: It's white, it's flat—the perfect canvas upon which to paint a perfect me. It's where I drive over bridges without closing my eyes or walk into elevators without bottles of vodka under my arm. It's where I whisk through book tours, answer reporters' questions, and make guest appearances on television shows without breaking into a cold sweat. It's where I board planes without downing Xanax and where I go on live radio shows without spending hours doing deep-breathing exercises beforehand, which never work anyway.

" 'Dear Randy . . .' " Dr. Gupta begins.

Only today, there's an intruder on my ceiling.

" 'I adopted a dog from you two years ago, and . . .' "

It's a little yellow spider who wanders back and forth above my head.

" '. . . his barking is starting to wear on me.' "

And if he loses his grip, he'll land right on my face. I close my eyes and concentrate on Dr. Gupta's voice—only I can't stand the thought of suddenly feeling a spider fall on my face without seeing it coming first, so I open them again and stare at the tip of my nose instead.

" 'He barks if someone knocks on the door. He barks at the mailman. He barks if he sees another dog walking past the house. He also barks when he wants to go outside and come back in. Like I don't know he needs to go out? And it's not so much that his barking is incessant. It's the sound of his woof. It has a high pitch, and I'm afraid he's going to cause me to have a seizure because the tone really hurts my ears. I will need to bring him back today. Please let me know what time I can drop him off.' "

When Dr. Gupta finishes reading, he clears his throat. "And what is it about this letter that upsets you?"

I want to scream, "Are you serious? She wants to return a dog *because he barks*!" Instead, I say, "I get dozens of these letters every month."

"And?"

"And, they're pretty much all the same. They are either too loud or too aggressive or too timid. They don't listen, and they make a mess of everything."

"And?"

"And . . . and then they get old and can't control their peeing."

"Yes, but isn't that behavior to be expected from these types of dogs?" Dr. Gupta asks.

The spider stops, spins in a tiny circle, and stops again. He's now directly above my eyes. Then he freezes in place and looks down at me. Slowly, as if testing the air before a free fall, he lifts one leg off the ceiling.

I'm not waiting for him to fall—or jump. With the fluidity of a marine in the enemy's crosshairs, I cross my arms tightly over my chest, roll off the couch and across the floor, and propel myself up onto a chair directly in front of Dr. Gupta's desk. I smooth my hair and pretend nothing just happened.

"I'm not talking about the dogs," I say as I wipe carpet fuzz off my face. "I'm talking about the *people*."

In all fairness, 90 percent of the people who adopt dogs from Stray Rescue know what they're getting into. Our crew specializes in saving feral dogs—those born on the streets who are as wild as coyotes but not as smart—and dogs who've been abused and then left to fend for themselves. Sometimes we spend years tracking an individual dog through the urban wilderness—watching his movements, his personality, the status of his position in whatever pack he's part of—and when the time is right, when he's so physically and emotionally weak that he'll surrender more easily, we trap him and bring him home.

Once a dog is in our shelter, our veterinarians address his physical needs, which tend toward broken bones, gunshot wounds, and strange things in their stomachs like wire and tin-can lids eaten because of starvation.

The second stage of the rescue focuses on socialization. The feral dogs who've never been touched by humans have one set of problems, while the abused dogs, the ones who've been used for sport fighting or for guarding crack houses, have another.

The feral dogs, for instance, must learn how to live in a house with people who love and protect them. These dogs tend to latch on to only one person, however, and because the bond is so strong with just that one person, they usually have problems with shyness and separation anxiety. It's almost impossible to get them on a leash or into a car at first, and they freak out when anyone turns on a vacuum cleaner, a garbage disposal, or a hair dryer. When their one person leaves their presence for any reason, these dogs howl like sirens to bring them back, and when that doesn't work, they'll tear through any barricade, including wooden doors and fences, to follow them.

The abused dogs, on the other hand, must learn that human beings won't hurt them, and their issues usually center on aggression, fear biting, and escaping from a life spent trying to avoid pain. These are the dogs who eat cats, the neighbor's poodle, and your most important dinner guests, and who've learned how to jump any fence, break any leash, or bite any hand that constrains them.

Our dogs, in other words, have *serious* issues. When we finally adopt them out to people who fully understand what problems might arise, we stick close with advice, trainers, and overall support. I have yet to receive a "return" from those who really love and understand their complex new companions.

Sometimes, once in a great while, there's a dog so screwed up that we can't in good conscience adopt them out. Those are the ones who come and live with me. I inhabit a house *full* of emotionally disturbed dogs. But I'm suited for them, because my own "issues" include what Dr. Gupta calls anxiety disorder, which means (in my mind, anyway) that I'd rather hang out in a house full of emotionally disturbed dogs than in a mall full of emotionally disturbed people, who, in general, spread ill will and germs.

Dr. Gupta used to say that I should be more understanding of people who wanted to return dogs they adopted from Stray Rescue, because not everyone was as "gifted" (his euphemism for "crazy") as I was. When I explained how much time, money, and emotional energy went into rescuing each and every dog, and how galling it was to have someone return the dog because she "gets in the garbage" or "licks the baby's face," he'd just lean back in his chair and say something like, "You are afraid to touch escalator handrails, and yet you'll let a dog lick your face."

"Yeah . . . so?"

"You are afraid of spiders but aren't afraid of aggressive dogs."

"And?"

"Well, some might consider that a bit of a contradiction. . . ."

"I'm not talking about *contradictions*, Dr. Gupta. I'm talking about people who return dogs because they *bark*. Did they expect them to sing 'The Hallelujah Chorus' every time someone knocked at the door?"

It wasn't until the day I brought him the following e-mail that things began to change:

Dear Randy,

You talked with my wife, Darla, a couple of weeks ago about Copper, a dog we adopted from Stray Rescue. Please contact us as soon as possible to make arrangements for her to be returned to your organization.

Copper is a very dominant alpha female. Sometimes it's either her way or no way. We have had her for about a year and a half. She has blended in with our family very nicely.

We think she is about three or four years old. She is protective, which we appreciate; she gets along real well with our boys and other dogs, and has a playful side that she doesn't hesitate to show. (There were some times in the past where she tried to enforce her dominance over me to the point of not allowing me to get into my side of the bed at night. She also refuses to let us cut her nails to the point of snapping at Darla. With all the dogs we have ever had, we have always brushed them and clipped their nails with no problems.) There is nothing physically wrong with her. She is healthy and not overweight. She is developing a beautiful coat and is otherwise a good dog.

We have never abused her and have
taken care of her in a responsible
manner, with regular trips to the
vet, exercise, and love. We are not
interested in a behavioral analysis.
As I stated above, I appeal to you to
please take her back. Perhaps she would
be better off on a farm or something
like that, but at any rate, I will no
longer put up with these incidents.
    Sorry, Randy; we tried to make it
work out, but the situation has gone
beyond what we think is a reasonable
attempt to straighten her out.
    Sincerely,
    David Dump

After Dr. Gupta read the letter aloud, I lost my cool and bellowed, "WHAT'S WRONG WITH THESE PEOPLE?"

Dr. Gupta's eyes lit up. "Look for the most obvious clues," he said. "The writer uses the phrase 'very dominant female' followed by 'she tried to enforce her dominance over me,' and 'I will no longer put up with these incidents.' "

"Misogyny?" I suggested.

Dr. Gupta nodded. "Or cerebral narcissism, probably stemming from issues with his mother. . . ."

"Do you think he dresses like a woman?"

After that, Dr. Gupta spent a great deal of time analyzing the e-mails, letters, and stories I brought him in an attempt to help me understand that I wasn't the only person with issues. In fact, he and I sat hunched over the letters and dissected them like coroners searching for clues.

"This one," I'd say rolling my eyes, "wants to return a dog because it's 'not cute anymore.' "

"Hmmm," Dr. Gupta said. "Craves novelty. Needs stimulation. Becomes bored with routine. Probably a histrionic personality disorder."

Or I'd say, "This one says her dog sheds too much," and he'd smile, shrug, and say that it was a classic symptom of obsessive-compulsive behavior, as if I should have known.

We even pored over research that connected animal abuse with domestic violence, including a 1997 survey of fifty of the largest shelters for battered women in the United States, which found that 85 percent of the women said pet abuse also occurred in the family.

While our informal little forays into the connection between a person's mental health and his or her treatment of animals stimulated Dr. Gupta and justified my frustration, it did nothing to solve the actual problem. I couldn't very well tell people who wanted to dump their dogs because they barked that they should see a psychiatrist instead.

Or could I?

"Probably not appropriate," Dr. Gupta said.

But I had to do something. We were dealing with *lives* here. These dogs were family members who had emotional needs, felt most secure when part of a family pack, and experienced an array of emotions including pain, loss, joy, and depression. Dogs are basically no different from four-year-old children. Their ability to learn is about the same; they eat with gusto, they love to be cuddled, and to play, play, play. The only difference between humans and dogs is their native language.

And so I wrote this book.

For practical purposes, it teaches folks how to correct their dog's "bad" behavior based on the years of experience I've had with dogs who act "badly." Each chapter includes a real letter or e-mail that I've received from would-be dumpers, and whittles the problem down to an easy solution.

Based on the kinds of dogs we adopt out, you might think that most of the letters would focus on dramatic events, like, "He ate the Girl Scout" (not the Girl Scout cookies—the actual Girl Scout). The truth is, though, that most of the dog problems people write to me about are the same problems all families with canines face: basic behavioral issues that are easy to solve, including peeing in the house, barking excessively, and running away.

For less practical (and for entertainment) purposes, this book acts as a catharsis for me and hopefully for the thousands of other shelter workers who must euthanize more than 27,000 animals *every day* in this country—that's 1,000 animals destroyed every hour, mainly because they overturned garbage cans or woke up babies with their barking. While most of my psychological prognoses about the letter writers are tongue-in-cheek, I think there's a little bit of truth in each one.

Immanuel Kant once said, "We can judge the heart of a man by his treatment of animals." As the founder and director of Stray Rescue, I say, "We can judge the personality disorder of a man by his treatment of animals." And in this book, I do so freely.

CHAPTER ONE

A.D.D. Dogs

```
Dear Randy,
    We adopted Annie from your shelter
about six months ago, and I'm afraid
it's just not working out. She's a good
dog overall, but she's so hyperactive
it's driving my wife and me crazy. In
short, we never realized how much work
getting a dog would be, and we think
it's in everyone's best interest if you
could find her a more suitable home.
    Please let us know when we can bring
Annie back to the shelter.
    Sincerely,
    Couch Potato Man
```

```
Dear Couch Potato Man,
    If you wanted a dog who sat next to
your wife on the couch and watched tele-
vision, you should have gotten a Gund.
They are soft and cuddly, and don't need
to be walked.
    Yours,
    Randy Grim
```

Against my better judgment, I didn't send that note. But this is what happened: Couch Potato Man brought Annie straight to the shelter with the complaint that she was "too hyper to live with," and in retrospect, now that the other dramas of that particular day are resolved, I feel a little bad about how I responded.

It happened to be one of those days.

The evening before, one of the dogs in the shelter went into labor, and because she was still recovering from life on the streets—malnutrition, dehydration, and a nasty wound on her neck—I spent the entire night in mucous-drenched shredded newspaper trying to make sure everyone popped out okay. They did—all seven of them—and while seven healthy newborn pups might be cause for celebration in some quarters, in mine it meant I'd have to find seven new homes in addition to at least 300 others.

On top of that, my assistant Jenn and half the volunteers all called in sick with the same flu, and without them, it's impossible to run the shelter. Especially if it's me that has to run the shelter. Jenn had instructed me to never answer the phones (something to do with being "rude"), so I didn't know how to deal with all the flashing lights on the new system. Jenn had also told me never to touch the new Mac (something to do with being a PC person and thus "stupid"), so I couldn't figure out how to turn it on. And no one had ever showed me where we keep the coffee filters, the extra toilet paper, or the paper towels (which I desperately needed to clean up the mess I made when I used toilet paper as a coffee filter).

On top of all *that*—and this is the big one (and the reason I suspect everyone called in sick with "the flu")—the day before, someone had brought us a little terrier he'd found on the side of the highway who had very obviously been sprayed by a skunk. The minute he stepped through the door, the sulfuric, satanic smell engulfed the entire shelter, and throughout the rest of the day, it permeated our clothes, the other dogs, and, I swear, my cigarettes. During every break I took, I inhaled skunk. To make matters worse, the terrier was friendly and rambunctious and kept jumping up on us, wanting to play.

Jenn Googled "skunk smell" and found that the best way to get rid of it was to bathe the terrier in vinegar douche—only no one would go to the store to buy the twenty bottles we needed.

"What would people think if a girl bought twenty bottles of douche?" Jenn asked.

"What would they think if a big gay guy bought twenty bottles of douche?" I asked.

"Just wear sunglasses," she said.

"*You* wear sunglasses," I said.

"I can't. I think I'm coming down with the flu."

So as the phones rang, the coffeemaker overflowed, and dogs who needed homes barked for their breakfast (which I couldn't find), a very rotund Mr. Potato plods in with Annie and says, "She's too hyper to live with," followed by a confused grimace and, "Jeez, what's that *smell*?"

I glanced down at the dog. She was of medium height and had a short white coat speckled with black and brown spots, which meant she was probably the result of a pet Dalmatian or Australian shepherd who got loose while in heat and then mated with a mixed-breed bad boy from across the tracks. Dalmatians, Australian shepherds, and other working breeds— including setters, pointers, retrievers, and spaniels—are dogs who've been bred for high energy, which means that they and any of their mixed-breed offspring will drive everyone around them crazy. Dalmatians, for instance, were selectively bred by the English aristocracy to run alongside and underneath their horse-drawn carriages. Why, I don't know (probably to guard their jewels or something), but imagine how much stamina it required for a dog to run under a coach for long periods of time at the same speed as the horses.

Terriers, too. Jack Russells, Scotties, Airedales, and any of their offspring who inherit some or all of their tenacious little genes will go out of their way to annoy you.

As Mr. Potato stood there waiting for me to say how sorry I felt for him, Annie's heritage betrayed her as she wrapped herself around his legs until the leash tightened, then unwound herself and immediately re-wound in the opposite direction.

"She never sits still," he said.

I nodded.

"She paces around the house constantly. It drives us insane. We have wood floors and her toenails click on them like I don't know what, a typewriter or something. We have to turn the TV volume up high to drown it out."

I nodded again.

"And then there's the barking. She barks at everything. She paces from one window to the other and barks out of each one. If the air conditioner turns on, she barks. If she sees her shadow, she barks. If a doorbell rings on the TV, she barks."

As if on cue, double lines on the phone started ringing, and Annie broke into song.

"See? And then there's the other stuff. Like when we walk in the house, she goes absolutely crazy, jumping up and down and gouging us with those toenails, yipping and yelping. Jeezus, it makes us crazy. We tried to teach her to sit, but the closest she ever comes to the actual position is a crouch, and then she just crouches there, shaking, like her energy's about to make her explode. Watch this. . . ."

Mr. Potato told Annie to sit, and she immediately danced in circles, crouched for a split second, then went spinning into circles again.

"See? And then there's the whole issue of demanding attention. We can't watch TV without her jumping up on the couch, trying to get in our laps and whipping her tail around in our faces. When we make her get down, she sits there, shaking, pushing her nose into our hands or walking back and forth, rubbing her body against our legs . . ." He inhaled, exhaled, and shook his head down at Annie, who upon eye contact jumped up and down at his side.

Mr. Potato looked at me expectantly.

"Do you know anything about Macs?" I said, pointing toward the white blob on the desk.

While high-energy dogs may not seem like a good match for people who like to watch TV, I propose that they are actually the *best* match for people who like to watch TV, because people who like to watch TV probably need the exercise more than their dogs. It's a win-win situation.

It's also a no-brainer. *Walk the dog.* Walk the dog for at least thirty minutes every single day. These dogs *need* to work to stay mentally sound, and if you can turn the walk into a jog, even a slow one, so much the better for both of you. If and when I run the world, high-energy dogs will only be assigned to qualified people—either those who drive Land Rovers with ski racks on top, bike racks on the back, and a kayak or two strapped to the roof, or those involved with agility and tracking competitions, dogsled races, or herding sheep.

As Mr. Potato slid his hands around the Mac, looking as I had for a button, *any button*, to turn the thing on, I looked down at Annie who pranced and paced at my feet. Her eyes swerved from Mr. Potato, to me, and back to Mr. Potato, as if pleading, "Yes! Yes! Tell him! Tell him! Sheeeeeeepherding!" But I figured the conversation would go thusly:

> **Me:** You know, Annie may have some Australian shepherd in her. Have you ever considered sheepherding or agility competitions?
>
> **Him:** (*Blank stare*)
>
> **Me:** Uh, how many walks does Annie get every day?
>
> **Him:** (*Another blank stare*)
>
> **Me:** Tell you what—let's do a little experiment. There's a drugstore about two blocks down. You and Annie walk down there at a brisk pace, and when you arrive, go in and buy twenty bottles of vinegar douche. Then walk back.
>
> **Him:** (*Blank stare tinged with suspicion*)
>
> **Me:** And get a receipt.

Because so many people complain to me about their "hyper" dogs, I've heard just about every excuse imaginable concerning why they don't walk them. "I just don't have time," is probably the number-one whine, but I don't consider that a good-enough excuse. You have a dog; get off your couch and *walk her*. I will make some concessions for "bad knees," "seasonal allergies," and "miscellaneous," which can include house arrest, a fatal reaction to bee stings, and living in harsh environments like the Arctic Circle.

A very good alternative for daily walks—maybe even better—is a Frisbee. For those with energetic dogs—walked or otherwise—this little disc is the greatest invention since the shoe. In fact, there are entire clubs and competitions revolving around canine disc sports, with names like the UFO World Cup Series (www.ufoworldcup.org), Sky Houndz (www.skyhoundz .com), and Yankee Flyers (www.yankeeflyers.com). There is even an International Disc Dog Handlers Association (www .iddha.com), which sets standards for competitions and titling and keeps track of record holders.

If you've ever seen one of these competitions, you may have noticed that most of the dogs look similar to yours—i.e., they are working breeds or mixed variations thereof, like border collies, retrievers, terriers, and cattle dogs. You may have also noticed that when they're racing across the field toward the airborne disc, they look like the happiest dogs on earth, which indeed they probably are, because running, jumping over obstacles, and leaping high into the air are activities they were *born* to do.

This is also an excuse-proof alternative, because once your dog learns to bring the disc back, all you have to do is place your recliner next to an open window.

I taught one of my own dogs, Steffi, to fetch a Frisbee, and it worked like a charm. Steffi was a terrier mix we found roaming the streets who was so energetic, we couldn't adopt her out. Someone whom she stayed with once e-mailed me: "So, does Steffi normally enjoy doing backflips off the ceiling?" Steffi was so hyper that every time I let her loose in the backyard, she ran around and around along the same oval path until my yard looked like Churchill Downs in no time at all.

When I first taught Steffi to fetch a disc, she had trouble concentrating on what she was supposed to do, so I started by rolling the disc like a wheel across the floor and then went wild with joy when she chased it. I made sure she understood that the only way she got to play the game was if she brought the disc back to me.

Once she got the fetch idea, I took her outside, bent down at her level, and tossed the disc a few feet in front of me—again, making sure she understood that she must bring it back if the game was to continue. At first, she waited for the disc to land on the ground before she picked it up, but as the tosses got farther and farther away from me, she accidentally jumped up once to catch it, and when she did, I went wild with praise.

Once Steffi had learned to leap up and catch the disc in mid-flight, I was so happy that I took the training no further. I just stood on my porch every morning, drinking coffee and throwing the disc across the yard for thirty minutes until she was so tired, she came back into the house a sane animal. So if you want to take the next step and teach your dog aerial tricks and cool sequences, you'll have to check in with the pros. Look at some of the Web sites I listed earlier for online advice, or Google "disc dog clubs" to find a group close to home.

"Found it!" Mr. Potato cried as the orchestra inside the Mac struck its opening chord and the screen came to life.

Sadly, I couldn't picture Mr. Potato even throwing a Frisbee, so I thought of suggesting a simpler alternative—putting twenty tennis balls in a pillowcase and tossing them across the yard for Annie to chase—but imagined the conversation would go thusly:

> **Him:** I'm sure my doctor wouldn't let me do that.
> **Me:** Why not?
> **Him:** Rigor mortis.

As one of the phone lines rang and then another in sequence, I asked Mr. Potato if he could figure out how to answer them and then walked Annie back to the holding area where thirty dogs were barking for their breakfast. Not one kennel was empty, and most were doubled up as it was. As I walked down the aisle trying to figure out where Annie could stay, anger—the kind with sharp teeth—got hold of my scruff and wouldn't let go.

It wasn't that we already had too many unwanted dogs in need of homes, or that most of them came from the streets where dozens more waited for rescue. It wasn't that I needed to make my daily rounds of abandoned warehouses to feed our stray packs, or that I should have trapped the starving mama dog whose puppies might be dead already. It wasn't the dog we found burned alive or the chow bald with mange or the pit bull at the vet's office with a bullet in his hip. It wasn't the constant, nagging need for more money, more volunteers, more foster homes, or more publicity that fueled my anger. It was simply this: *How could someone give up their dog?*

Then I heard the smelly terrier yelping from the confines of the supply room where we had stashed him solo for the night. Annie heard him too, and with the force of a mule team pulled me toward the door. Meanwhile, up front, Mr. Potato answered one call after another, frantically scribbling messages on the back of a Speedy Burger bag he'd pulled out of the garbage:

1) CALL LAURIE SOMEBODY ABOUT SOMETHING

2) Foster dogs got in fight. CALL BOB? Bill? Ben? ASAP. 233-67??

3) Vet's office: Rotwyler Rotwiller Rotwhyller with neck wound doing better—German shepherd (with chain embedded in neck?) is OK—two spays and three nooters done this morning—pit bull with gunshot died last night.

4) Policeman, said he was friend, raided dog-fight ring. Needs help with six dogs, several in bad shape. Is on his way here with them!

5) Mindy. Volunteer. Says she and someone else out feeding packs and caught the starving mama dog and three puppies. Is on her way in with them now. Says to get a kennel ready!!!!

6) Lady named JEN says she got the doosh. Wanted to know why I was answering phones. Told her I DON'T KNOW.

When I came back to the front, fully intending to give Mr. Potato a piece of my mind, he ran toward me, shoved the Speedy Burger bag into my hands, stammered something about needing to "get ready," and looked wildly around the room as if he'd lost something.

"Where's my Annie?" he said. "Where *is* she?"

"Uh . . ." I pointed to the back in confusion. He grabbed Annie's leash from my hand and followed the direction of my finger.

I glanced down at the bag and barely had time to sigh before Mr. Potato rushed back into the room followed by an exuberant Annie and an equally exuberant stinky terrier on Annie's leash.

"What . . . ?"

Mr. Potato waved his hand back and forth at me to quell any questions. "Never mind—there's no time. They're on their way here."

He headed for the door with both dogs.

"Wait," I called, but he didn't even look back at me, just said something about Annie needing a friend. He didn't even close the door behind him.

Turns out, sometimes all an energetic dog needs is another energetic dog to keep them company. Several days after Mr. Potato had disappeared with the stinky terrier, he returned to the shelter with a smile of relief, a large donation check folded inside a thank-you note, and a scrap of paper covered with his handwriting.

The look of relief, he said, was because Annie and Flower played so much together, they wore each other out. They smelled to high heaven because he couldn't get the skunk smell off but he figured it was a small price to pay for domestic tranquility.

"And, Annie's happy," he said.

The donation check and the thank-you note were for the "great public service" done by Stray Rescue, which Mr. Potato said he'd never understood until he answered our phones. "After taking all those horrible calls, I ran out of room on the bag and grabbed this," he said and then handed me the scrap of paper on which was scribbled the following message: 7) LADY HAS HYPER DOG. WANTS TO BRING IN. "After calls about gunshot wounds and dog-fighting rings and starving mamas and puppies, this lady calls and complains she has a hyper dog. I wanted to tell her to go to hell, because there were dogs losing their lives out there . . ."

"So what *did* you tell her?" I asked.

"That she had the wrong number."

I nodded my approval, wadded the paper into a ball, and lobbed it with grace into the garbage can.

"Wait here a sec," I said, then went in back to search for the twenty bottles of vinegar douche that Jenn had bought at the store.

Happy Ending/Quick Fix Recap for Hyper Dogs:

- Walk the dog every day.
- Buy twenty tennis balls, put them in a pillowcase and throw them across the yard for the dog to retrieve.
- Alternatively, teach the dog to catch a Frisbee.
- Consider adopting a companion for your energetic friend.

CHAPTER TWO

The Escape Artists

Hi Randy:

   I adopted a wonderful bully mix from the pound a year ago. She was a six-month-old stray that was injured and wasn't going to last long there. She has been sooo sweet to our kids and our other rescue dog.

   We have had two incidents in the last two weeks where she has gotten out of the house and jumped on neighborhood children. We have been asked to find a new home for her, and we are devastated.

   Would you be able to help me find a wonderful home for Sadie? She is house-trained, fun, energetic, lovable, and cuddly. She's got the cutest little tail wag you ever did see.

   Sincerely,
   Dolly Dumper

Dear Ms. Dumper,

I know exactly what's going through your head. You are the bad neighbor, the one everyone is whispering about, because you have an uncontrollable mixed-breed rescue dog instead of a gooey-eyed yellow Lab, which makes the neighbors question your genetics, your child-rearing abilities, your team spirit, and your social IQ.

But this is really about your inability to stand up to the neighbors. Read on.

Sincerely,

Randy Grim

I can just hear the neighbors: "Pretty soon, they'll have truck tires, abandoned refrigerators, and rusty RVs in the front yard . . ." and you, Dolly Dumper, alone will be responsible for lower property values, higher neighborhood death rates, and declining school test scores because your uncontrollable mixed-breed rescue dog jumped on the neighborhood children and traumatized them so much, they can no longer do arithmetic. So you hide in your house and pray for a worse neighbor to move in.

Believe me, I know. You're talking to a guy who lives in a gentrified urban neighborhood and has *several* mixed-breed rescue dogs, one of whom has to wear a wire-basket muzzle, like Hannibal Lecter, just to be within 100 feet of any other human besides me.

Charley doesn't take kindly to strangers. I rescued him from a pit bull fighting ring, and while he loves *me* to death, he wants to devour strangers with a nice Chianti and some fava beans. (It's not his fault; I place the blame on the Michael Vicks of the world who think organized dog fights are fun sport. Someday I'd love to introduce Vick to Charley, sans muzzle. I'll bring the Chianti.)

Charley has certainly done nothing to boost my social standing among the neighbors, who've invested whole retirement accounts to update the turn-of-the-century houses we live in. While I'd like to say that I don't care what they think about me and my mongrel horde—which has turned my backyard into a muddy Sahara—the truth is that I do. I'm just so far gone in their eyes, it's all I can do to keep from being tarred and feathered.

So picture this: It's a rainy spring morning. I've just woken up, and I'm standing at the kitchen window on the second floor in my underwear, sipping coffee, looking down on the backyard and admiring the brand-new $5,000 privacy fence I had constructed to placate the landscape divas on either side of me who claimed Charley "scared" them.

Charley's out there taking a dump in the rain, and I'm about to call him in when I see a Ford Escort tear down the alley behind the house, followed closely by a police car with its lights flashing. Just as my brain registers what's going on, the Escort veers, skids on the wet pavement, and then plows straight through the back of my brand-new fence.

And right into Charley's yard.

The last thing I remember clearly about the pursuit that ensued was the wide-eyed masked bandit running *toward* the police with Charley, in his wire-basket muzzle, not far behind.

The rest I can only imagine, and I now obsess daily about what my neighbors saw running past their windows that morning: A terrified guy in a ski mask, followed by a terrified policeman in uniform, followed by a large dog in a wire-basket muzzle, followed by yours truly in his rain-soaked underwear, screaming, "Charley, *sit!*"

Charley wasn't brought up on attempted murder charges that day, but had I not been the director of the only no-kill animal shelter in the city, I too might have considered dumping my seventy-pound would-be serial killer in someone else's lap.

Instead, I called my therapist, Dr. Gupta.

"Have you ever heard of Wilfred Trotter?" Dr. Gupta asked after I'd told him how worried I was that my neighbors saw my butt crack when I finally tackled Charley and lugged him back to the house in the pouring rain.

"Exhibitionist?"

"No, a neurologist and social psychologist who coined the phrase 'herd instinct' back in the early 1900s. He compared the human need to be part of a group with that of a dog whose 'terror of loneliness' gave it the 'capacity for devotion to a brutal master.' "

"And . . . ?"

"And, people stick with the crowd because it's safer than being on their own," Dr. Gupta said. "They will believe, submit, and do almost anything to be part of the herd."

The trick—which *is* a trick if you're as socially phobic as I am (I've hosted parties I did not attend)—is to understand and use herd instinct to your advantage.

So I went home and called my neighbors.

"We've *got* to do something about crime rates," I said before they could demand that I get rid of Charley. I then quickly suggested organizing a neighborhood watch group, demanding more streetlights from the city, and encouraging "our neighbors" to all get dogs like Charley who would scare away criminals, and, in extreme cases, like this morning, help the police track and apprehend them.

To a person, my neighbors applauded the idea.

You, Ms. Dumper, are terrified of rejection by the herd, which is understandable, because every human being, deep down, wants to be cool. It's instinctual. The problem in this situation is that you're *so* insecure about your status that you'd give up a friend who's a little in the wrong. Just how much respect do you think that will gain you in the end? If you don't get rid of the apologetic, groveling, just-wipe-your-shoes-on-me attitude and start acting like a herd leader, dumping little Sadie will be the least of your problems. Once the pack establishes you as its most-inferior member, even the way you prune your azaleas will come under group scrutiny.

Now I'm not talking about fake leadership—you know, the kind where you act like you think a leader should. Once, when my rottweiler/mastiff mix escaped and galloped into a neighbor's backyard party, sending the guests running before devouring the abandoned chicken on the barbecue, I responded to their hysteria with a fist-pounding, "DOGS HAVE RIGHTS TOO!" This did nothing to help the deteriorating relationship and nearly landed me in jail. So I'm not suggesting that you bang the table about your place at it.

Instead, act cool, very cool, and establish in less than ten minutes who is superior to whom. First, bring the neighbor some store-bought cookies (heated in the microwave and put on a plate to give the illusion of homemade) and then commiserate with her about her children's fear-of-dogs *neurosis*. Make sure to use that word. No parent wants a neurotic child who will repeat everything to a psychiatrist twenty years down the road. Then suggest that the kids might get over their *neurosis* if they help you walk Sadie every day, and if that doesn't cure their *neurosis*, you will, as a superior neighbor, build a fence to keep Sadie in her own yard, which won't cure the kids' *neurosis* but will keep them out of an institution for at least a few more years. Finally, gossip about some other neighbor to take the spotlight off you.

Then, go get the big yellow phone book out of the hall closet, open it up to the "F" section, and turn each page until you see the following sequence of letters: F-E-N-C-E. Pick one of the numbers, any will do, and then dial it. When someone answers on the other end, give them your credit card number and your address.

Do *not* say anything else. Do not go on and on with the fence person about what a bad neighbor you are, or about your uncontrollable mixed-breed rescue dog, or about the "cutest little tail wag you ever did see," because the fence person will immediately peg you as a—let me grab the thesaurus to find a more tactful word for "pushover"—as a "ninny," and will consequently take advantage of you and charge an arm and a leg.

If you really can't afford a fence, consider some good old-fashioned dog training. Sadie, as well as your neighbors, needs to understand who steers the ship.

First, teach Sadie to sit for everything and *anything* that she wants. To do this, place a food treat on her nose. Then raise the treat over her head so that her eyes will follow it and her disobedient little rump will fall to the floor. As soon as this happens, immediately give her the treat.

Then, whenever Sadie wants anything—to be petted, fed, played with, let outside—she must sit first. This automatically becomes a habit, what Dr. Gupta would call a "default behavior."

So if Sadie regularly escapes the house by bolting out an open door, for example, teach her to sit-stay by the door when people are coming and going. Before you teach her to be trustworthy, keep her in another room or crate, (see chapter 14 for crate-training lessons) away from the door, to anticipate and avoid opportunities for escaping.

If you look at this problem from Sadie's point of view, running away is rewarding. She gets to do all kinds of groovy things like chase squirrels, smell whatever she wants, and jump on the neighbor's children. Even if she isn't strictly running away, you are probably like many other dog guardians who let their pooches do their own thing while off lead, and only call them back when it's time to put the lead on and go home. This doesn't encourage a dog to want to come back to you, since it means fun time is over.

As with your neighbors, you must use a little Machiavellian cunning and a few treats to get the results you want.

Happy Ending for Escape Artists

- If your dog doesn't come to you in the house when you call her, she sure won't do it when she's outside playing. Start at home, then, where you have no traffic or other dogs to worry about if she ignores you.

- Walk her only on the lead for a while. If she pulls, a head collar will give you more control.

- Put some hard tidbits in a small plastic box or bottle, so you can rattle them. Keep them in your pocket around the house, and three or four random times a day, rattle the container. Call Sadie to you at the same time, and give her lots of praise and a tidbit when she arrives. Get everyone in the family to do the same. Sadie may look at you as if you're mad at first, especially if you wake her up, but stick to it. That rattling sound will soon mean food.

- Do this when you are in the same room at first, and then try it from another room so she has to come and find you. Make sure it's a fun game with lots of love and praise.

- Don't give her any food at any time (tidbits or meals) unless she responds to a recall command first. Always recall her to have her lead put on, to be groomed or patted, or anything else nice. Give lots of praise and a tidbit when she comes. All of this helps her associate pleasure with coming when called.

- Always take her out when she's hungry, preferably just before a meal, as this makes the tidbits more tempting. Take plenty of tidbits with you in your usual container. Cut her meals down to allow for this—I don't want the blame if she gets overweight. It doesn't matter if she gets, say, a third of her daily food like this at first; you can taper it off later.

Play the calling game whenever you're out, even though she's on a lead. Call her every few hundred yards, praise her, feed her, play with her—make a big game of it. Do this on the street, as well as where you normally let her off lead. This should make her start keeping one eye on you all the time.

In conclusion, when you take a dog into your family, she becomes a real member of your family. As tempting as it may be to just dump her at times, remember this responsibility, and your life—and your dog's—will be richer as a result.

And, like me, you'll probably get a few good stories in the bargain. Like, one time an ice storm knocked out the electricity for several days, and I had to take Charley with me to the swankiest hotel in the city. . . .

Quick Fix-1

Dumping Excuse: "I am moving."
Quick Fix: Good for you. Take the dog with you. If your new apartment won't allow pets, find one that does. This is where I can't fix stupid.

CHAPTER THREE

Dogs Who "Play" When You're Away

Dear Mr. Grim:

    Phoebe, the dog we adopted from you, has destroyed our home. You assured us before we adopted her that she was a "sweet dog," but she has turned out to be a manipulative and vindictive animal who seeks revenge every time we leave the house.

    In the two months since we adopted her from you, she has shredded or peed on everything in our house, including (but not limited to) our carpeting, our furniture, our shoes, and our beds. Our neighbors say she howls when we're gone.

    We now understand why she was available for adoption in the first place.

    Not only will we be returning this animal to you, but we have also contacted our attorney regarding restitution.

    Signed,

    Mr. and Mrs. George Wrathful

Nothing sends me to Dr. Gupta's couch faster than the words "we have contacted our attorney," and after hours of comprehensive cognitive-behavioral therapy and a one-year renewal of my Xanax prescription, he advised me to redact so many sections of my response to Mr. and Mrs. Wrathful, and this is all that's left:

```
Dear Mr. and Mrs. Wrathful:
    Sincerely,
    Randy Grim
```

But to set the record straight, Phoebe was not a "manipulative and vindictive animal" who sought "revenge" every time the Mr. and Mrs. left the house. Rather, Phoebe suffered from separation anxiety, common with many abandoned dogs—which meant that every time her new family left her alone, she went crazy with fear: She defecated in the house, howled, scratched gouges in the doors, and chewed up anything she could get her teeth into (like I do every time I quit smoking).

If your dog displays any of the following behaviors, then she's probably afflicted with separation anxiety:

- Behavior occurs *only* when you aren't home: defecating, ripping at curtains or blinds, scratching up doors, and chewing on clothes, pillows, blankets, or towels.

- Neighbors tell you she howls when you're gone.
- Your dog seems hyper-attached to you when you are home (i.e., she follows you from room to room and begs constantly for attention).

In a majority of cases, separation anxiety occurs in dogs who come from pounds or shelters, or who suddenly find themselves, for whatever reason, living with a new family. It also happens sometimes when a dog's routine changes. If, for instance, you move to a new house, you go from part-time to full-time work, or even when there's a divorce or death in the family, your dog may go through a short period of freaking out.

Over the years, I've dealt with hundreds of dogs who suffer from separation anxiety. I've had dogs destroy homes within six hours of adoption, and I've paid thousands of dollars for repairs, painters, carpenters, and entire cleaning crews so that strays don't take a bad rap.

One of my own dogs, Hannah, ate six pairs of shoes and ripped my best suit to shreds the first time I left her alone (I went to buy cigarettes—a *seven-minute* trip). After that, I crated her when I left, but every time I came home, she was still standing outside her crate, surrounded by piles of poop, torn-up papers, and something—usually something expensive—still in her mouth.

One evening, after putting Hannah in her crate and securing it with chains, plastic wire, and a bicycle padlock, I attended a party in the park by my house and invited some people over for drinks when it ended. As usual, Hannah had escaped, greeting us at the door with a pair of my shredded underwear in her mouth. Beyond her, in the bowels of the living room, lay the worst of her destruction yet: the rest of my dirty laundry; the contents of the kitchen garbage can, including coffee grounds, eggshells, cigarette butts, and dirty little secrets like Ho Ho wrappers; the feathers of three down pillows; the couch cushions; an unrolled roll of toilet paper; and the dirt from a large potted palm, which had turned to mud after she'd added some water from her water bowl. In addition, she'd overturned a can of lime-green paint in the basement and then tracked it all the way upstairs. To this day, Hannah's paw prints still grace my living-room floor. People think it's art.

I never did figure out how Hannah escaped the crate, by the way. There were never any visible signs of how she did it. The first time it happened, I called the police because I thought someone had robbed me and for some reason, maybe to be mean, they'd let Hannah out in the process. I now attribute it to UFOs.

In Phoebe's case, we found her limping down the middle of a residential road, skeletal, flea-ridden, and practically bald from mange. When I knelt down and called to her, she limped right over to me, which meant she wasn't a wild or feral dog but a scared and confused pet abandoned by her family, and from the looks of her, *long* abandoned by her family. This in turn meant that she suffered mentally as well as physically, because pack animals who lose their packs lose a part of themselves.

Dogs, like wolves, live for their packs. From the minute mama wolf pops her pups out, the pack dictates every move they make—when they eat, where they sleep, whom they play with, what they think—because the pack structure, fair or not, keeps individual wolves alive. Everything in a wolf pack, from raising pups to hunting food, requires cooperation. For example, when wolf pups are born, the job of the mom, the alpha female of the pack, consists of protecting and feeding the pups in the den, while the job of subordinate members includes bringing food to the mom in the den. When the pups grow old enough to leave the den, they're "placed" in a rendezvous point by the older wolves who meet there periodically during the day to check on the pups or bring them food. By the time the pups are about six months old, they learn the pack's hunting techniques, which in and of themselves involve cooperative tracking, signaling, and ambushing among all pack members. If one of the wolves is injured during the hunt, the others usually bring him food until he recovers.

Over the millennia, we've managed to cull many of the physical characteristics of wolves from dogs—put a pug in front of a wolf and he'd probably eat it—but we've never bred out the pack mentality. It's instinctive. It's a need. And for a dog whose pack consists of humans, it's a matter of survival. Dumping a pet dog in the park is like expelling a wolf from the pack; unless she finds a new pack, she will probably die a lonely death in a relatively short period of time, and will do anything, submit to anything, to belong once again.

In Phoebe's case, as with any dog abandoned—or in their minds "expelled"—from the pack, the experience is so frightening that even if they find the safety of a new family, they suffer a sort of post-traumatic stress. Dogs like this are so afraid of rejection that they often hyper-attach to their new pack members. As a result, every time they're left alone, they experience abandonment all over again. Terror grips them. Hoping they're only temporarily lost, they howl so the pack can find them again. When that doesn't work, they claw at doors to get out, so they can go and find the pack themselves. When that doesn't work, they become so afraid that they lose control of their bowels and tear blindly at anything holding the pack's scent, including pillows, shoes, and blankets.

Whatever you do, DON'T PUNISH THE DOG when you get home. Her behavior isn't so much destructive as it is desperate, because she feared you abandoned her. Remember always that a dog has about as much chance of surviving all alone as a four-year-old kid. In his book, *The Ecology of Stray Dogs*, Alan Beck noted that the average life span of a family dog is 10.5 years, while the average life span of a stray dog is 2.3 years. I've not kept records, but in all of the years I've spent tracking feral dogs (those born wild on the streets), I've never seen one with arthritis. So when you walk in the door and find your shoes with teeth marks, your coffee table books ripped to shreds, and the legs of your sofa splintered like fireplace kindling, DON'T PUNISH THE DOG. I can't stress this enough. DO NOT PUNISH THE DOG.

Since the cause of separation anxiety is fear, the cure is security. The problem is that you can't just lavish your dog with love, hugs, and diamond-studded designer water bowls, hoping she'll equate this with security. She won't. She's addicted to you and will always need more.

Now, I'm no fan of anything that doesn't bring instant gratification—if a meal doesn't meet my three-step rule in which step one reads "peel back lid and place in microwave," and step three says "enjoy," I don't buy it—so let's make this easy on ourselves and think of the cure for separation anxiety as a simple one-step process, which is: FOLLOW DIRECTIONS THAT FOLLOW.

(This exercise may seem a little silly at first, but remember— you can't convince your dog verbally that you'll be back. You must communicate with her through actions she can understand and interpret.)

- Start by **putting on your coat** in front of the dog (even if it's hot) and **grabbing your keys.** She'll probably show all kinds of distress like whining, barking in your direction, and circling around you. Ignore her, say nothing to her, and then sit down at a table or any place where she can't jump up on you. Sit there until she calms down. Then stand up, take off your coat and put the keys away, still ignoring her. Repeat this chicanery several times until she stops acting crazy.
- Now, **put on your coat, grab your keys, walk to the door, and open it.** Again, she'll probably get all upset, and when she does, sit back down and wait for her to chill. Repeat until it doesn't bother her anymore.
- Next, **put on your coat, grab your keys, open the door, and step outside.** Leave the door open so she can see you, and immediately step back inside and sit down. Repeat as necessary.
- This time, **put on your coat, grab your keys, open the door, step outside, and wait a few seconds.** Then come back in, sit down, and ignore her. The idea here is to get

her used to not seeing you for a few seconds at a time with the full expectation that you will return. Lengthen the time you stay outside from seconds to minutes, and always ignore her when you come back in.

- Once she understands that you always come back from the other side of the door, it's time to teach her the verbal cue. Now, each time you **put on your coat, grab your keys, open the door, and step outside, you say, "Long live the king."** You could also say, "I'll be back" or something, but I always say, "Long live the king," because I'm extremely superstitious about my health. Whatever the cue is, always use the same one. Do this several times, always returning within a few minutes and sitting down.

- Finally, you're ready to increase the time you remain on the other side of the door, so **put on your coat, grab your keys, grab an adult beverage, open the door, step outside, saying, "Long live the king," and stay outside for longer and longer periods of time.** Each time, return and sit down.

- Now here's the part I didn't want to tell you about earlier: You must repeat this whole process every time you leave for at least a week. It's a headache, I know, but it will eventually work. Think of it as house-training a puppy: It's time-consuming in the beginning, but well worth the effort in the end. Try to make it fun for yourself; have a friend outside to talk to, enjoy an adult beverage, buy a Game Boy or an MP3 player, and just enjoy being outside. Don't worry about the fact that your neighbors are watching you walk in and out of the house with your winter coat on in the summer; wave like they are the crazy ones. (It's also great for dealing with human kids who don't want to go to daycare.)

Once your dog understands that you aren't abandoning her every time you leave, reinforce her sense of security by leaving her an article of your clothing to smell and the TV or radio on. Better yet, buy a Kong toy at the pet store and leave it with her. This is a hard, plastic toy you stuff with treats, which by design are tough to get out and keep your dog's mind off the fact that you aren't around. Hannah enjoys a Kong stuffed with peanut butter (that I froze overnight, like a Popsicle) and now runs to her crate when I grab my keys.

While this training works with 90 percent of all dogs, there are some who have such severe histories of abuse and abandonment that nothing works but drugs. I'm a big believer in better living through chemicals. I myself use . . . well, a lot of medication prescribed by Dr. Gupta, who, exasperated with my lack of progress on the couch, said a bunch of heady stuff about the lack of serotonin in my brain and neurotransmitters doing this and that, but ended with what I consider a plausible excuse: "If it works, why not?"

Currently the only two medications for dogs I know of are clomipramine and fluoxetine, which both work well. According to one of my veterinarians, they produce feelings we humans might associate with eating chocolate or falling in love, which tempts me at times to try them myself. Talk to your vet if you want to go this route.

As for poor Phoebe, who suffered abandonment twice, we placed her with a foster family that patiently worked through her problems with her. They tell me that she shows no more signs of anxiety, and that she'll live with them forever.

(*Note to Self*: Consider writing a book about family relationships, including crating some family members during the holidays with a gingerbread-stuffed Kong.)

CHAPTER FOUR

Shuuut *Up!*

Dear Sir,

    I adopted a dog from you about two years ago. Max is a great dog and I love him dearly, but his barking is starting to wear on me. He barks if someone knocks on the door. He barks at the mailman. He barks if he sees another dog walking past the house. He also barks when he wants to go outside and come back in. Like I don't know he needs to go out? And it's not so much that his barking is incessant. It's the sound of his "woof." It has a high pitch and I'm afraid he's going to cause me to have a seizure because the tone really hurts my ears.

    I will need to bring him back today. Please let me know what time I can drop him off.

    Best,
    Duh

Dear Duh,

    Did you originally think dogs meowed?

    Dogs, for the record, bark. Most of them bark a lot, and if they're anything like one of my dogs, Stinky, they bark at absolutely nothing.

    Best,
    Randy Grim

S tinky, a stumpy little yellow pit bull, barks at rain, new art on the wall, his empty food bowl, piles of laundry, and birds. Sometimes he sits in the middle of the backyard and barks at air. One night, while loading the dishwasher after a dinner party, I dropped a fork on the floor and Stinky went nuts. When one of the guests asked with panic in his voice what the dog was barking at, all I could do was shrug and say, "A fork."

Stinky is only one member of the pack that inhabits my house, and his barking usually sets the others off en masse. If I'm on the phone and, say, a large mosquito flies past the front window, I can't even hear myself yell "I HAVE TO CALL YOU BACK" into the receiver, which is especially embarrassing if you're being interviewed on a live radio talk show. One time I listened to a tape of one of these radio interviews, after it aired—but all that could be heard was a lot of barking and me screaming, "SHUT *UP!*"

The second Tuesday of every month is the worst. That's when the city tests its weather sirens, and the dogs stand at the front window and howl like a pack of wolves in the Grand Tetons during a full moon. The second Tuesday of every month is the *only* time my neighbors venture near my house because they want to make sure "everything is all right."

Several years ago, a reporter from a national magazine asked if she could interview me "in my own environment." She suggested my house. I suggested an abandoned parking lot on the far south side.

At first, I thought Stinky in particular barked to get attention. See, dogs evolved from wolves, and while adult wolves don't bark, wolf pups do. It's the equivalent of a human baby crying to get his mother's attention, because he doesn't yet know how to communicate in any other way. So the wolf pup barks until he learns how to communicate in adult-wolf ways.

But over the millennia, humans have selectively bred wolves into mere shadows of their former selves, and the result—dogs—are really just adult wolves physically, and wolf pups emotionally. In other words, dogs are big babies looking for attention.

Stinky, for instance, would sit in the middle of the backyard and start this *woof-woof-woof* thing while his head turned slowly from side to side like he was sending out warnings to anything that *might* be in the general vicinity. My first "command" through the window was always a well-reasoned, "There's nothing there, Stinky—hush," which usually worked until I stepped away from the window and he'd start again. *Woof, woof, woof.* We'd go back and forth that way . . .

Me: Stinky, *please* be quiet.
Stinky: (silence)

Me (turning away from the window): Good boy.

Stinky: Woof, woof, woof.

Me (back at the window): I *said,* be *quiet*.

Stinky: (silence)

Me (turning away from the window again): Good boy.

Stinky: Woof, woof, woof.

. . . on and on, back and forth, until my inner hick lost control and was heard throughout the neighborhood bellowing, "FOR GOD'S SAKE, SHUUUT *UP*," through the window. Usually in a bathrobe.

Here's what was happening: Stinky barked to get my attention, and when I yelled at him, he just thought I was barking back. Mission accomplished. I was *rewarding* him for barking. The answer, then, was as simple as *not rewarding* him when he barked. I started inside the house. When he barked at anything that wasn't a burglar, I pulled out a plastic water sprayer and gave him a little squirt. He hated it, and within several weeks, he managed to put two and two together.

If a person has one dog, the water sprayer works great. I, however, have an entire herd, and after a while I developed carpal tunnel from pulling the trigger so many times. That's where a good, old-fashioned dog whistle comes in handy. If the crew starts barking, just blow the whistle, which hurts their ears and pulls their attention away from whatever they're barking at. This is a good way to make them shut up when they're outside too. The only problem with this method is that during dinner parties, with the dogs locked away in bedrooms, you sit at the table and blow continuously into a silent (to humans) whistle. If you don't want your guests to see you blowing into a whistle, just place it in your napkin and pretend to wipe your mouth, blowing all the while. They will just think you are a messy eater with perfectly behaved dogs.

Many dogs—especially those like ours who were either feral or abused and thus tend to attach to only one person—bark when their person leaves the house. It's the only way they know to call them back. There are a couple of easy solutions for this, though.

Quick Fix for Too Much Barking

- Get another dog to keep the first one company;
- Turn the TV or radio on, so they don't feel so alone;
- Use a bark collar; or
- Ask your veterinarian about medications for separation anxiety.

The bark collar is probably the most practical solution, especially in multi-dog homes, because it works whether you're home or not. I'm not talking about a shock collar here. Not only does it physically sting the dog, but if you have as many as I do, it knocks out whole sections of the national electricity grid when they go off in unison every time the dogs bark.

Instead, consider a citrus collar. Dogs hate the taste of citrus, and every time they bark, the collar ejects a spray of citronella onto their muzzles. I love this method for entertainment value alone, because you've got a pack of dogs at the window on the verge of warning you there's a car driving by, and suddenly, at the very first *woof*, they go silent with puckered lips, their tongues darting in and out, giving each other quizzical looks as if to say, "Do you taste that too?" The citrus collar also saves you from buying air fresheners.

There are also ultrasonic collars that, much like a dog whistle, emit a high-pitched sound people can't hear, and collars that vibrate every time they bark.

If you want to avoid the expense of bark collars, it's easy to improvise. Get a tin can, put twenty pennies in it, and shake it every time the dog barks. Likewise, put lemon juice in a spray bottle (rather than water) and squirt it at his mouth when he woofs, and you'll not only have a quiet dog but a good laugh as well. (You can also use it on your fish for dinner.)

Whatever you do, don't talk, pet, or try to soothe your dog with your hands when he's barking. This only tells him you love him for driving you crazy. Only reward him when he *doesn't* bark at something he normally would, which I know is difficult when, like Stinky, your dog barks at drying paint, growing grass, and forks. Try it anyway.

In the end, a person really can't get too upset about barking. There are so many people out there, from politicians to spouses, whom you'd love to squirt with lemon juice or place inside a shock collar, that a little barking from the dog shouldn't seem so annoying. I think it is because we spend all day listening to the rants of others, and by the time we get home, we feel we can finally scream SHUT UP and not worry about being arrested. In my house, I only reprimand nuisance barking. If the doorbell rings, I tell my crew, "Go on, let it out," because I wish so much that I could.

Quick Fix-2

Dumping Excuse: "My boyfriend doesn't like my dog."
Quick Fix: Dump the boyfriend.

CHAPTER FIVE

The Turd Eaters

Dear Mr. Grim,

    About three months ago, I adopted from your organization. She's very loving, even though we've had to deal with her being very shy and unsure of most situations. She seems to be happy; however, she will not stop eating poop. She's eating our other dog's poo from the yard, and also doing her best to keep our litter boxes cleaned. It's so disgusting; we just can't deal with it. Last night we found a turd in our bed. For my husband, it was the last straw . . .

    Sincerely,
    Doody Dumper

Dear Doody,

    Obviously, she left the turd in your bed as a gift, because if she liked the taste of poop, she would have *eaten* it. I'm curious: Was it a cat turd or a dog turd?

    Yours,
    Randy Grim

will confess to two things at this point (and only because Dr. Gupta says that I should):

1) I'm not sympathetic enough with people who haven't read as many self-help books as I have and thus can't handle the eating of turds, and,

2) despite the number of self-help books I've read, the thought of eating turds makes me want to hurl.

I admit, it *is* pretty disgusting. I saw one of my own dogs, Ichiban, do it once—ran up to another dog pooping in the yard like he was the ice cream man offering free treats—and I couldn't even look at him for an entire week.

At first, I did my usual: drank a little wine, went into denial, and pretended it never happened. Everything was fine for a while, but then early one morning, as I stood at the kitchen window sipping hot Brazilian Robusta, watching the dogs play in the backyard and, in general, feeling that all might indeed be right with the world, Ichiban did it again—he wolfed down poop as it came hot out of the other dog's butt, and my rare moment of tranquility (along with a mouthful of Brazilian Robusta) splattered against the wall.

One of my biggest phobias (of which, admittedly, I have several) is of germs. It's a generic kind of fear—germs in general scare me—and I avoid public bathrooms, escalator handrails, handshaking, and all-you-can-eat buffets. I flush *my own* toilet with my foot. During the course of my lifetime, I have visited the emergency room with symptoms of the plague, botulism, bird flu, tuberculosis, West Nile, malaria, and anthrax poisoning.

I nearly had a nervous breakdown once when some friends, playing a practical joke, left a message on my voice mail from the "Federal Department of Infectious Diseases and Emergency Sanitation," saying they had "reason to believe" I'd come into contact with someone who carried streptocophal, an extremely rare and potentially lethal disease, and that a special "contamination vehicle" had already been dispatched to my residence to take me to a nearby air force base where I'd be "administered special tests" which included an anal probe. I fainted on the spot.

Needless to say, giving Ichiban mints wasn't an acceptable solution for me.

When I mentioned the situation to Dr. Gupta during one of our sessions, he leaned back in his chair and nodded his head slowly as he always does when a more-interesting issue than my phobias comes up.

"Coprophagia," he said.

"Is that some sort of ancient war cry?"

"It's a Greek term," he said, "from *copros*, which means feces, and *phagein*, which means eat."

"Sounds like a war cry to me."

"It's not all that unusual in some species, and in rare cases, even human beings engage . . . "

I plugged my fingers in my ears and hummed. I couldn't afford more therapy.

It turns out The Condition (which is what I'll call it from here on out because I can't pronounce or spell the technical term) is not so rare in dogs. Some theories suggest boredom, stress, parasites, or digestive deficiencies as the cause, but in most cases, The Condition starts when the dog is young and then becomes sheer habit.

Sometimes it begins with a puppy or dog who simply likes to pick up objects and carry them around. During cold weather, for example, a puppy might find a frozen turd on the ground and think he's discovered a great toy; then, as he carries it around in his mouth, it starts to melt and . . . you know . . . resemble food.

Snow is another factor. There is nothing more exciting to a young dog than sniffing out something that smells like food under a dusting of snow, and their hunter-gatherer instinct loves every second of it. So be diligent when the weather changes so this doesn't start to become a habit.

Other first steps include the following:

- Visit a veterinarian for a health check to make sure there are no signs of parasites.
- Make sure you are feeding your pet a nutritional dog food.
- Pick up the stools so the dog does not have access.

The most important factor when you first notice The Condition in your dog is to take immediate steps to prevent it from happening again. Behavior modification techniques are your best hope. For example, always take your dog out on a leash at first. Whenever she starts drooling over a found turd, use a corrective sound (like your mom used to make when you were drinking from the milk carton), like the direction *leave it*, and then give an alternative command such as *come*, *sit*, or any direction that will take the dog's attention away from her snack.

In addition to behavior modification, the following also works:

- In many cases, there are particles of undigested food in feces, which might be what's bringing her to the table. Add enzyme supplements such as meat tenderizer or papaya extract (a natural enzyme available in health food stores) to her food to increase digestion.

- Add two to four tablespoons of canned pumpkin to her food each day, because while it's acceptable when it goes down, it's distasteful when it comes back out.

- There are products such as Forbid and Excel available from pet supply stores and veterinarians that discourage The Condition. Apply the product directly to the turds. Apparently, it tastes horrible.

- Finally, try Randy's Tequila Lime Turd Spray, which when used on poop acts as a deterrent, but when sprayed on grilled fish (swordfish or halibut are best) acts as marinade. Whatever you do, don't label it TURD SPRAY like I did and then use it while preparing dinner in front of guests.

> ### *Randy's Tequila Lime Turd Spray*
> 1/2 cup lime juice
> 2 Tbs. tequila
> 2 cloves garlic, minced
> 1 tsp. Tabasco
> 1/4 cup chopped cilantro
> 1/2 cup olive oil
> Salt, pepper, and paprika to taste
> Combine all ingredients in a glass container. Store in the refrigerator.

In the end, poop doesn't have to be the enemy. You may just have to learn to deal with it: Look the other way, don't accept a wet kiss from the culprit for twelve hours, or, use the marinade. Come on—we've all woken up next to someone whose breath smells as if they have The Condition. Give your dog a break here, and me too.

CHAPTER SIX

Cujo in the Dog Park

Hi Randy,
    Can you give me some advice about what to do with Peaches? She's a basset hound mix, and she attacked a golden retriever yesterday at the dog park and almost killed him. This is the third time she's done this, and she's already been through several rounds of professional behavioral training, so I was thinking of having her teeth taken out as a last resort. What do you think?
    Thanks,
    Witless Wally

Dear WW:
    What do I think? Here's what I
think: Anyone who lets a dog-aggressive
dog in a dog park should be tarred,
feathered, and put on public display.
I think anyone who lets wicked Rover
run loose in a dog park should then be
required to wear a big red "S" on their
clothes, for STUPID, take some sort of
medication for stupidness, and attend
stupidity awareness classes for the rest
of their natural lives. That's what I
think.
    Sincerely,
    Randy Grim

Does it actually take a mental giant to realize that any dog with aggressive tendencies shouldn't be allowed to run loose in a dog park? I love all dogs, so don't get me wrong. Many dog-aggressive dogs have the best sense of humor of any dog I've dealt with, and love their human companions with a bighearted stubbornness that borders on obsessive. But that's the problem: When these dogs want something, they obsess.

Case in point: I got a call from one of our volunteers, a young guy named John, who fostered one of our more-abused rescue dogs named Blue. John told me I needed to get to his house ASAP because, as he put it, "Man, there's something really wrong with this dog."

When I pulled into his driveway, John stood by a fence with several of his neighbors who waved me toward them as they stared into the backyard with looks of horror on their faces. I, of course, expected the worst, and as I ran toward them, pictures of Blue with the last remnants of a FedEx delivery person's uniform hanging from his mouth flashed through my mind.

(When you work with as many street dogs as I do, you come to expect those sorts of things. Once, a hysterical volunteer who was fostering one of our dogs called me in the middle of the night, and all I could understand through her incoherent crying was MAX . . . *sobs, gulps for air* . . . KILLED . . . *more sobs, more gulps for air* . . . PERSON. At least, that's what I thought she said. What she actually said was MAX KILLED PERCY (her cat), but because I always expect the worst, my mind translated it into MAX KILLED PERSON, and subsequently I had a lot of explaining to do to the police, detectives, paramedics, and firefighters who showed up at her house after I called 911.)

What I saw when I reached John's fence was not the actual worst, but it ranked high on my list of potentials. In the backyard stood an old tree with low-hanging branches, and underneath one of the branches, Blue circled with a franticness that indicated prey up above. As I searched the tree for the FedEx guy, Blue suddenly sprang up toward the branch, grabbed it in his jaws, and then held on and *hung there* like a dangling wind sock, six feet off the ground.

"Oh wow," I said. "Who's in the tree?"

John shrugged and shook his head with that sad, resigned look reserved for the hopelessly insane. "No one."

I looked back at Blue, who still hung from the branch. "Is it a cat?"

"No, man, there's *nothing* in the tree."

"But . . ."

"Yeah. Weird, huh?"

For whatever reason, Blue was so obsessed with killing the tree branch that whenever John let him out in the backyard, he jumped up, grabbed it, and hung on for up to five minutes before he'd let go. Then he'd drop down to the ground, circle a few times, and repeat the attack all over again.

"He'd do this all day long if I let him," John said. "He'll hang on until his gums bleed."

That is how obsessive some dogs are, and when you throw in abuse (like a fighting ring), you'll start to understand why they should never be allowed to run loose with other dogs who could, and often do, end up being the object of their obsession. I have had countless aggressive dogs, and many can love and play well with others; it's more a matter of what people did to them before I ended up with them and their "issues."

I can hear you now—"I *paid* for this advice?"—but if you have a dog-aggressive dog and insist on letting him hang out with other dogs, then you are one of many who needs something akin to electroshock therapy when it comes to common sense. It's like dealing with a person who has a false sense of entitlement.

I am not saying that all dogs who show aggression toward other dogs can't be taught some manners (see below), but no matter how much you work with him, if he's aggressive toward other dogs, you can never fully *trust* him around other dogs. Sounds harsh, I know, but that's the sneaky point of this chapter: It's not about training your dog to like other dogs, but about teaching him a few points of social etiquette (see Grim's Guide to Proper Introductions below), and about you accepting and dealing responsibly with your dog's personality (see Grim's Guide to Proper Fork Use, on page 84).

Grim's Guide to Proper Introductions

Typically, dogs show one of three types of aggression toward other dogs—dominance, territorial, or fear—but regardless of the triggers, a few general rules apply to all:

1) If the dog is not spayed or neutered and you aren't willing to spay or neuter them, then you must wear the big red "S" on all of your clothes—see Randy's letter on page 74.

2) Invest in a halter-type collar—they give you much more control than a regular collar, including choke chains. Never let the dog out in public or around other dogs in the house unless he has it on.

3) Teach your dog to "sit," which won't cure the aggression, but will allow you some control in certain situations.

4) Teach your dog "stay," which, again, won't cure the situation, but will give you an extra tool.

5) Invest in a basket muzzle for working with your dog in public.

Unfortunately, in my line of work, I run across the extremes. Many, many of the dogs we rescue are either former "bait" dogs used to train the fighters (and thus fearfully aggressive), or the fighters themselves (and thus aggressive on dominant or territorial grounds). I won't go into all the horrible details, but I bring it up because I've never met a dog more fearful than a former bait dog or more aggressive than a former fighter, and in both cases we've been successful in introducing them to polite society and with a higher success rate than that achieved by our current penal system.

Fear Aggression

The symptoms of fear aggression in a dog include barking and nervousness when he sees other dogs, backing away from other dogs with his tail between his legs, pulling his ears back horizontally, looking away from the other dog, and raising his fur. The good news is that this is the most treatable form of dog-on-dog aggression. The bad news is that you have to read chapter 8 to fully understand the treatment.

Here, however, is a condensed version: You must gradually teach your dog to relax around other dogs, and to do this, you should start with teaching him to relax when you ask him to "sit." So start there—teach him to sit and to *relax*.

I emphasize the word *relax*, because you are not actually concerned with teaching your dog to sit, but with teaching your dog to relax. To do this, take the dog to a safe place where there aren't any other dogs, and ask him to sit. Then, wait for him to relax, and when he does, give him a treat. I suggest the canine caviar, hot dogs. Repeat this over and over in different place where there are no other dogs. Remember—you are trying to teach the dog to relax, not to sit, so he must believe the two go hand in hand if he's going to get his treat. Every time you ask him to sit, he must associate happiness and relaxation with doing what you ask.

Once he makes the association of sitting/relaxing with groovy treats, take him outside, preferably to a park where there are other dogs, and practice the sit/relax from a distance. It's really important not to get too close to the other dogs at this stage, because you don't want your dog reacting to *them*;

you want him reacting to *you*. So, take him to the park, and when he sees another dog in the distance and starts to whine or bark, ask him to sit, and don't give him his treat until he focuses on you and relaxes. Whatever you do, don't baby or reassure him when he whines or barks at the distant dogs, because this in effect teaches him that it's okay to act that way. Just distract him by asking him to sit.

It may take several days or several weeks, but when your dog can be relied on to relax in the presence of distant dogs, start moving closer and closer, repeating the exercise in exactly the same way. What you're doing is counterconditioning him to his fears, teaching him to respond to his fear in a way that doesn't involve aggression, and once he gets this into his head, you're ready for the final step: his introduction to polite society.

The introduction should take place in the park, or wherever you worked on the counterconditioning. Ask a friend with an already-polite dog to meet you there. Then walk the dogs (on leashes!) side by side, but keep the distance between them wide enough so they can't reach each other. While there may be a few snarls at first, keep walking side by side at a brisk pace, and within one lap of the park, your dog should show relaxed behavior. If and when you're comfortable with it, walk them a little closer together, and then closer still. As long as you walk quickly and with purpose, there should be no problems, and eventually, maybe over the course of only a few days, your dog and your friend's dog will be best buddies.

Repeat this exercise with other dogs, but never let either dog off leash. Do not let what appears to be a miracle fool you. It will only take one wrong whiff by another dog to set your fearful one off.

The worst thing you can do is take your dog to the dog park—on leash or off. If he's on his leash and other dogs swarm around him, he'll feel trapped and lash out. If he's off his leash and other dogs swarm around him, he'll still lash out, but you won't have any control over him.

So when *can* he run loose in the dog park?

Skip down to Grim's Guide to Proper Fork Use for the answer.

Dominance and Territorial Aggression

Aggression caused by dominant attitudes or territorial protection share similar symptoms, including fights between dogs in the same house and aggression toward strange dogs, with the bad guy (your dog) staring the other directly in the face, with his ears forward and his tail raised before he goes for the throat.

When you walk them through the park, these are the guys that make all kinds of noise when they see other dogs, and lunge and twirl on the end of their leashes like hooked marlin on the end of a fishing line. These are the guys who act like they're going to crash through the front window of your house when another dog walks by. These are the guys who embarrass you in the car, at the vet's office, and in those pet store chains where you can bring your dog, because people wonder what you did to make him so mean. You, in fact, are probably wondering what you did to make him so mean. I can't count how many times someone called or wrote me with the following tearful lament: "I don't understand it. He's so gentle and sweet around people, but when he sees another dog, he turns into Cujo. What am I doing wrong?"

The answer is, probably nothing. If you aren't training a dog to fight other dogs (in which case you should be in prison), then the chances are good that it's part of the dog's makeup, especially if he has human-induced aggression or overbred bad-rap breeding running through his veins. These poor guys have been bred for hundreds and hundreds of years to protect *their* people from werewolves, rebellious serfs, and invading Huns, and whatever it is about the atoms that make up their cells that make up their genes, it just can't be bred back out in a generation or two.

So you have to trick your loyal protector of the castle in much the same way you'd trick a fearful dog out of being afraid: You teach him to sit using hot dogs (and no, Oscar Mayer has not endorsed this book).

I cannot emphasize enough the power of hot dogs. After considerable and methodically sound research, I have determined that they contain unique cataleptic properties similar in effect to humans snorting pure chocolate, and are, in my opinion, the single most persuasive dog-training tool known to humankind.

Start in places where he won't be distracted by other dogs, and teach him to sit using cut-up hot dogs as his reward for obeying. Like the fearfully aggressive dog, you are not really teaching him to sit, but to defer to you and then to relax. Repeat the exercise again and again until he automatically associates the word "sit" with hot dogs and happiness, and only then begin practicing in public.

Always keep him on a halter-type leash when you start the counterconditioning, because you must have physical control at all times. A regular collar—even a choke chain with prongs—won't do the trick. Take him to the periphery of a park where there are other dogs, and every time he spies one and assumes his I'm-gonna-kick-some-ass posture, tell him to sit. He'll probably ignore you at first, but wave a hot dog around in the air a few times above his head, and watch the offal-stuffed casing do its magic. Once he sits, wait for him to relax. Don't reward him if he sits and jitters, or sits and keeps looking back at the other dogs. Wait for him to sit, look up at you, and *relax*.

Once he does, give him his reward, and walk on. Then repeat, repeat, repeat.

As with the fearfully aggressive dog, the time for his social debut is determined by how well he learns to relax on command. If every single time you ask him to "sit," he obeys and looks up at you with the gooey expression of a stuffed panda, then you're ready for Grim's Guide to Proper Fork Use, below. If, however, there is any hesitancy on his part—if he whines, or fidgets, or averts his eyes toward the other dogs, for instance—then he's not ready and must continue his lessons. Desensitizing is the magic key here.

At this point, your question to me is probably, "Won't my dog get fat with all these hot dogs?" and my response is, "Yeah. So?" Would you rather have a fat, happy dog or a lean, mean killing machine? And besides, once you get through this chapter, you'll be able to take him jogging through the park to lose the weight without getting the usual dirty looks from parents of "normal" dogs.

This coincidentally leads me into the next section . . .

Grim's Guide to Proper Fork Use

Now that Cujo can go to the park and not act like a total redneck, he's ready for the final phase of counterconditioning, which, for him will be easy, because he won't actually have to do anything.

You, however, will. Don't worry, though, as there are only two steps.

Step One: Tell yourself that Cujo will never be able to run loose with other dogs, and once you're convinced, move on to Step Two.

Step Two: Reward yourself with a hot dog.

"But . . ."

But nothing. Cujo can now walk through the park with grace and civility, and for a dog who still probably wants to attack other dogs, that's a goal you should be proud he's reached.

"But . . ."

Get over it. As far as I'm concerned, the most proper way to use a fork is to scare away people with aggressive dogs who insist on letting them loose in dog parks. Any size fork will do. Believe me (because, unfortunately, I know), when someone with a crazy look in their eyes runs toward you screaming, "GO AWAY" while waving a fork, it doesn't matter whether it's made for salad or made for steak, you go away.

Look at it from their point of view. Their dog Dopey lives for the moment every day when the leash comes out and they head for the dog park. It gives Dopey's parents so much pleasure to give him so much pleasure that the three of them can barely contain themselves. As they approach the park, Dopey gets more and more excited, and when he finally sees his friends romping together across the grass, he all but loses his mind with joy. For his parents, there's nothing quite like bending down, unhooking the leash, and watching Dopey tear across the field toward his buddies, who in turn go nuts with happiness when they see him coming, because for that one little moment of every single day, all seems right in their worlds.

Then you and Cujo arrive.

Have you not noticed that everyone leaves when you and your mean dog arrive?

I know how much you love this dog and want him to be "normal." If he could just run and play with the others, you're sure he'd learn to adjust. I know how many books you've read and programs you've watched and Web sites you've scanned, and how many times you've tried, *really tried* to follow the advice, just to watch him fail again and again. After a while, you even get superstitious about it and wonder whether it has something to do with the food you're feeding him or the feng shui–ness of your house or some weird trajectory of an undiscovered comet zooming through the House of Pluto. Is there lead in his toys? Is his collar too tight? Does it have anything to do with his vaccinations?

I know your eventual conclusion like I know the palm of my own hand because, after you've disinfected his belongings, exorcised your home, hired a dog-behavior coach, put him on a treadmill, and purchased all-natural, made-in-America, free-range, gourmet food, you've decided, through a process of elimination, that it must have something to do with *you*. You are the problem somehow.

Again: Get over it.

Unless you're encouraging him to attack other dogs, it's not your fault, and no matter how polite he becomes as a result of hot-dog counterconditioning, no matter how sorry you feel for him, no matter how much you want him to have friends and be part of the gang, if a dog is aggressive toward other dogs—for whatever reason, and even if it's only once in a while—he cannot be trusted around other dogs.

One of the most frustrating parts of my work comes when I get calls or e-mails from people like Witless Wally who insist that their dogs are, deep down, just like the dogs in the dog park and that if he could only find the solution that keeps eluding him, everything would turn out okay in the end. But it won't, and it's one of the hardest realities for people to accept.

It might be easier, though, if you look at it this way: THEY DON'T WANT YOU IN THE DOG PARK.

If it helps, think of your dog as "haughty" rather than aggressive—so far superior to Dopey and the like that playing with them doesn't interest him in the least. The only reason he attacks them is because they're too dumb to understand.

Once you accept your dog for who he is, whatever mental gymnastics it takes, it's simply a matter of adjusting a few things in your life, and my job is done. First, be realistic about your dog and who he is, and love him like your mom is supposed to love you. If you countercondition him with hot dogs as explained earlier and can walk him down the street or through the park or into the vet's office without any scenes, then you've accomplished more than 95 percent of parents with aggressive dogs ever accomplish.

Second, learn and understand what triggers his aggression, and reject those triggers like handshakes during flu season. Dr. Gupta calls this "avoidance," and assures me it's okay as long as it doesn't involve taxes, oil changes, or relatives. So if dogs in the dog park set him off, you can avoid the dog park and not have your therapist accuse you of having an avoidant/borderline-mixed-personality disorder.

Third, if you live in a home with more than one dog, keep Cujo separated from the rest, especially when they eat, sleep, or run in the yard. Never leave them alone together, and don't feel guilty about it, because would you rather feel guilty about fencing them off or about one doing serious damage to the other? You can try a basket muzzle, of course, if the dog can live with it, but you still have to separate them when they eat. I still separate my crew when feeding. I do not recommend, however, taking a muzzled dog to the dog park, because Cujo may still attack out of habit, and because Dopey will naturally fight to defend himself, Cujo will be the one who gets hurt.

Quick Fix-3

Dumping Excuse: "The dog gets in the garbage."
Quick Fix: Uh . . . try putting the garbage can in a place where he can't get to it.

CHAPTER SEVEN

Dogs Who You-Know-What in the House

Phone message #1: Hey, Randy—This is John. Buster pisses on everything. Haven't heard back from you. Call me ASAP.

Phone message #2: Randy, you didn't tell us the dog we adopted from you isn't house-trained. I've left a couple of messages already. Thanks, Joanne

Phone message #3: Hi Randy, I've been trying to call you, but you never seem to answer your phone. I'm having problems with Leah, who pees on the carpet every time I leave the house. Call me, Terri

```
      To: Anyone who has a dog who you-
know-whats in the house
      From: Randy
      Re: House-Training
      I'm away for the next several years
and won't be checking my e-mail.
```

```
      From: Randy
      To: Jenn
      Re: Dogs who you-know-what in the
house
      Jenn—If anyone calls the main number
for me regarding a dog who isn't house-
broken, pretend bad connection and hang
up.
```

Just between you and me, I hate the urine issue. I hate the way it smells, I hate the way it sounds coming out, I hate saying the word or any euphemism thereof. I've searched the thesaurus for alternatives to "urinate," which I hate writing, and all I found were things like "pee," "piss," and "tinkle," none of which I will say out loud unless I'm drunk at a bar and trying to find a bathroom. The only possible substitute was "see a man about a horse," which makes no sense, but because this is the number-one bad-dog issue, and because every other message on my e-mail or phone has something to do with it, and because I can't get away with "Haven't you *heard?* Yellow is the new black," if your dog sees a man about a horse on your carpet, reach for the vinegar (see below), and take comfort in the fact that you aren't alone.

My house smells like salad, or what my Mom describes as "pickled beets." Between spraying lemon juice for barking, Tabasco for turd eating, and vinegar for the you-know-what, it's like walking into an Eastern European delicatessen, because my house is the victim of every known assault by dogs who see men about horses, including puppyhood, insecurity, territory marking, and separation anxiety. The thought has even occurred to me while doing the pee dance and rushing for the bathroom that I might as well see a man about a horse on the carpet myself, because everyone else has.

Puppyhood

In the good old days before I founded Stray Rescue, back when my biggest responsibility in life was maintaining a cool house and hip wardrobe, a skinny female dog followed me home through the park one day, and while I tried to ignore her as she limped along behind me, it was like ignoring a skinny stray dog limping along behind me. Guilt incarnate. When I finally reached my door and turned around, she sat at the foot of the steps and stared up at me.

I lit a cigarette and stared back. "What?"

She cocked her head.

"What's wrong?"

She cocked her head the other way.

"What do you want?"

She extended her front legs until her belly reached the ground. Then she laid her nose on her legs, rolled her eyes up toward me, and exhaled loudly as if exhausted from her trip and glad to be home. After considerable mental debate and three more cigarettes, I shrugged and invited her in. Why not?

Well, for one thing, she—Bonnie—was pregnant. She was as skeletal as a dinosaur on top, but from the sides, as bloated as the Goodyear blimp. It was like looking at Nicole Richie while pregnant.

For another, she delivered not one, not two, not five, but thirteen—that's THIRTEEN, as in a baker's dozen—puppies.

For yet another, Bonnie developed mastitis, an infection in her boobies, so I became a surrogate mother dog and bottle-fed the thirteen puppies 'round the clock for six weeks. In my sleep-deprived state, I often wondered if this would be my fate if I went to hell.

And then, as the puppies grew, so grew their bladders—and my budget for air fresheners. You can read all the nightmarish details in *The Man Who Talks to Dogs*, but for purposes of this book, imagine the conversation that took place between a sleep-deprived, freaked-out gay guy with thirteen little leaking monsters to take care of and his totally unaccommodating veterinarian.

"Why can't *you* just take them, Doc?"

"I sympathize with you, Randy, but you're simply going to have to house-train the puppies while you find them homes. You should never have bred her in the first place."

"How dare you call me a breeder . . . and I have to house-train *all* of them?"

"First thing in the morning, every morning, take them outside . . ."

"But—"

". . . and when they urinate, praise them—"

"But—"

". . . then, after they eat, wait half an hour and take them out again."

"But—"

"It's a matter of consistency."

If you are anything like me, the word *consistency* conjures up things like oil changes, sit-ups, and flossing, but nevertheless, you must face this ugly word when you get a new puppy. And if for some reason you have thirteen of them, it becomes, quite quickly, a profession. So I have no sympathy for those of you with just *one*.

The first thing you must do is set up a schedule and stick to it, and remember this: A puppy has no muscle control until she's about sixteen weeks old, so until then, subscribe to the *New York Times* daily and put it on the floor near the puppy. Seeing your puppy poop on politicians' faces will, at worst, brighten your day.

After that, a puppy must pee every hour that she is old in months, so if she's three months old, she can only hold it for three hours. I started house-training Bonnie's puppies when they were two months old, which meant that every two hours I had to take thirteen fat little balls of energy outside en masse. Only it didn't work out so well, because as soon as I let them out of their pen in the basement, they scattered like bowling balls in every direction, and I spent half the day retrieving them and then cleaning up the messes they accomplished while I was retrieving someone else.

So instead, I descended the basement stairs thirteen times, picking up a puppy thirteen times, ascending the stairs thirteen times, and taking a puppy outside thirteen times—and when they did their business, singing praises thirteen times. I figured out that during that time, I said "HALLELU-JAH!" 4,680 times, which *must* earn me some sort of high status in the afterlife, i.e., every time a puppy did his thing Randy earned his wings.

But after a while, I realized they were so attached to me that they'd follow me wherever I went, like ducklings follow a mother duck. I was so delirious from lack of sleep that it seemed to make sense for me to quack and flap, and they indeed learned that this was the signal for them to go outside.

I'm a big believer in crate training. (See chapter 14.) Dogs usually won't see a man about a horse in the space they sleep and eat in, and while puppies don't get it at first, eventually they'll come around. Just make sure the crate isn't too big, because the puppy will do her stuff in a distant corner and not be bothered. So keep your puppy in a crate at night, and first thing every morning—before you brew your coffee, have a cigarette, or see a man about a horse yourself—take the puppy out of the crate and to the backyard. Place your *New York Times* on the ground in the backyard, so the puppy understands that this is where to go. As soon as she does her thing, praise and pet her, so she associates doing the deed *outside* with pleasure.

Then, bring her inside and for about half an hour or so, let her play at will. Watch her, though, because as soon as she squats anywhere in the house, you have to screech and jump up and down (presumably still in your bathrobe and without caffeine in your bloodstream) so she conversely associates doing the deed *inside* with something rather hideous. (P.S. Most of my dogs have a fear of me in my bathrobe. Will tackle that issue in another book.) Between the screeches and the deed itself, make sure to brew your coffee because the work has just begun and you need to be awake.

After thirty to sixty minutes, put her back in her crate where you give her breakfast. When she's done eating, take her back outside and wait for her to do a number-two, which invariably happens about half an hour after she eats. Praise her, pet her, and bring her back in, then repeat the whole process over and over for the rest of the day. Be sure to stock up on staples that will help you deal with the stress of house-training your puppy (e.g., wine, chocolate, nicotine, and/or vodka) because here, in short, is your schedule:

- Take her out first thing in the morning.
- Playtime.
- Outside.
- Breakfast in crate.
- Have a Mimosa.
- Outside.
- Playtime.
- Have a cigarette even if you don't smoke. Trust me on this one.
- Outside.
- Lunch in crate.
- Have a Bloody Mary.
- Outside.
- Playtime.
- Outside.

- Eat an entire box of chocolate truffles.
- Dinner in crate.
- Take Valium. Call neighbor or pharmacist for supply. Tell them it's an emergency.

In other words, your life revolves around the little beast for about a month, after which time she should let you know when she needs to go out. Don't expect her to come up to you and say, "I need to see a man about a horse." Watch for signs: whining, circling, and sniffing, or what I call "the look." My Hannah, a mixed-breed street dog, is queen of "the look." She sits up and stares very intensely at nothing, her brow wrinkles up, and I know it's time for me to open the door.

If you work and can't watch the puppy closely, then you probably shouldn't have her in the first place, but since you do, put her in a crate when you leave and have someone—a dog walker, for example, or the neighbor who loaned you the valium—let her out *at least* once every couple of hours. It will take much longer for her to learn the rules this way, however, so be prepared.

As for Bonnie's thirteen puppies . . . the story ends happily. I found every one of them a good home. When I approached a potential adopter—in my bathrobe with a cigarette dangling from my mouth, a box of chocolates under one arm, a bottle of Visine under the other arm, a fifth of vodka in one hand,

and a puppy in the other—and asked for a light, they usually grabbed the puppy in horror and ran.

To this day, people still ask me why I didn't just ignore Bonnie when she followed me home from the park; or why, if I was so inclined to keep her, I didn't take her to the pound when I found out she was pregnant; or why, once the puppies were born and Bonnie developed mastitis, I didn't drop them off on the doorstop of my greatest enemy.

I have no grand answer. It wasn't Bonnie's fault someone abandoned her in the park, any more than it was the puppies' fault they were born in the first place—and besides, taking care of those thirteen puppies monopolized every waking thought, which left no room for self-centeredness, self-pity, or self-loathing, all of which, when allowed free reign, send self-confidence and self-fulfillment running for cover. It was *good* for me. It also led to the eventual creation of Stray Rescue. It changed my life.

During the chaos, though, people accused me of having a mental breakdown, as if I was an alcoholic in need of intervention, because I wouldn't take Bonnie or her puppies to the pound "like any normal person would." But the truth is, "any normal person" would have heard the same thing I heard when Bonnie limped behind me through the park to my front door—that inner nagging voice, which interpreted her look: *Please, don't leave me here.* And they would have ignored it.

But for once, I listened.

And now I always listen. Just ask Dr. Gupta.

Territory Marking

Recently, I entertained a short-term guest in my home—a huge, old, un-neutered pit bull named Goober—who religiously marked all four corners of my bed each night before he jumped in.

I first saw Goober when I traveled to New Orleans with Jeff Popowich from Best Friends Animal Society in Utah (www .bestfriends.org) and a film crew from *National Geographic* to rescue dogs abandoned after Hurricane Gustav. We were part of a group of first-wave responders, and authorities gave us a partial list of dogs they knew were chained inside homes or to fences and then left behind. We worked from 6:00 AM to midnight every day for a week.

I found Goober lying on a sidewalk that led up to a house in which a woman stood and yelled for help. Turns out, Goober wasn't her dog—he'd just picked her sidewalk to rest on—but he was arthritic and weak from hunger and thirst. He could barely stand up anymore, let alone walk away. He was a large pit bull, with ragged ears, fighting scars, and testicles the size of baseballs, and that convinced the woman inside that he was laying there waiting to eat her.

Jeff and I managed to get the old guy inside our rescue van, and despite his pain and weakened state, his tail banged like a bongo on the van's metal floor. He was that grateful. Needless to say, I decided Goober had probably lived a hard-enough life already, so instead of transporting him to the local shelter, which was already overloaded with abandoned dogs, I brought him back with me to the evacuated vet clinic that served as our makeshift home during the rescue operation.

The short walk from the van to the door of the abandoned clinic took us half an hour, because, in addition to limb-numbing sores and arthritis, Goober, like any un-neutered alpha male—canine, human, or otherwise—had to mark every blade of grass along the way, even after he was empty and nothing came out. It's a territorial thing, like a Wise Guy leaving a calling card, and no matter how inconvenient it is, no matter how much it slows down business, one doesn't yank Tony Soprano by the chain.

Once we made it to our temporary bedroom (a floor and a sleeping bag), Goober peed all over the place: the crates, the operating-room table, the corner of my backpack on the floor. When I finally climbed into my sleeping bag and patted an invitation to him, Goober first hobbled from one corner to the other, making his mark, then, with painful slowness, he climbed up next to me and made himself comfortable.

For dogs like Goober, marking isn't just peeing—it's an instinctual drive. Researchers argue about why they do it—to intimidate intruders, to maintain territorial borders, or to make a map for themselves so they don't get lost—but no matter the reason, they still do it, and it still smells bad. At least to us. Dogs don't think peeing is as gross as we do. In fact, if an alpha male lifts his leg over the mark of a subordinate female, he's basically telling her he'll protect her no matter what. It's a compliment.

Dogs are really nothing more than learning-disabled wolves, and scent marking in a wolf pack is one of the most important forms of communication. The alpha male in any wolf pack—the guy who leads the hunts, attacks intruders, and gets the females—does most of the scent marking, and does so most frequently at the edges of the pack's territory, to keep neighboring packs in their own 'hoods. Lone wolves don't even leave scent marks, because they don't want to attract unwanted attention.

So when you have an un-neutered male dog in your house, you basically have a dumb wolf who's play-acting. GET HIM NEUTERED AND HE'LL STOP. If you're one of those people who don't want an "emasculated" dog, there are fake balls called Neuticles (I kid you not) that are testicular implants your veterinarian can install that "allow your pet to retain his natural look, self-esteem, and aid in trauma associated with neutering." They come in various sizes and firmness—Original, Natural, and Ultra Plus—offered online at www .neuticles.com.

While un-neutered males are, like, a million times more likely to scent-mark than neutered males, even fixed dogs need to make their presence known sometimes.

My dog Quentin, for example, accompanies me on book tours for *Miracle Dog: How Quentin Survived the Gas Chamber to Speak for Animals on Death Row*, and despite his good manners and neutered state, he still marks the legs of anyone who stands too close to me. If I'm standing there talking to someone with Quentin sitting at my side, at some point he'll quietly step over to the person and pee on their leg as if telling them, "He [meaning me] is mine," and then he'll resume his position at my side as if nothing happened. The interesting part is that nine times out of ten, the person I'm talking to pretends it never happened either. (*Note to Self:* Ask Dr. Gupta why people who get peed on by Quentin feign obliviousness. Submissive? Starstruck? Stupid?)

Anyway, when I brought Goober back to St. Louis, he stayed with me for a few days while waiting for a space in our shelter. I had him neutered immediately, but he still marked anything vertical that didn't move, including furniture legs, floor-length curtains, grocery bags, plants—even blank walls and closed doors. Every night after he'd marked all four corners of the bed, and after I'd climbed out to wipe them off with vinegar, he climbed down too and marked them all over again. He marked the purses of donors, the tripods of photographers, and the boots of overnight guests who never came back. (I read somewhere that they mark vertical objects aboveground to ensure a large evaporative surface that in turn ensures a stronger odor.) Regardless, every time Goober drank at the water bowl, all I could think was, "He's not thirsty; he's just refilling."

It doesn't matter how old a dog is when he's neutered: The drop in testosterone will eventually change his instinctual drive to mark things, usually in a few weeks, from a need to a habit. In other words, if you have an un-neutered male dog who marks everything in your house and you don't have him neutered, then he will, in all probability, still mark everything in your house. If, however, you do get him snipped, it's simply a matter of breaking a bad habit.

The only way to start breaking the habit is to catch him in the act, and you must be diligent about this, because no matter how inconvenient it seems at the time, it will save you, your dog, and your furniture in the end.

If you are agoraphobic (afraid to leave your house) like me, it's easy: Tether your dog to you for two whole days, and every time he circles or sniffs, screech "NO MARK!" and immediately shake a tin can filled with twenty pennies. If you live with someone named Mark, you must use a different word, but whatever—the idea is to make the dog associate marking in the house with an awful sound that startles him and hurts his ears. Of course, follow up with praise or a *hallelujah*.

This is what I did with Goober. On the first night of training when he went to one of the bed corners and sniffed, I jumped up and bellowed "NO GO!" while shaking my can of pennies like Carmen Miranda in a high-speed salsa dance. Goober's leg dropped immediately and he stared up at me with a cocked head. When he shuffled over to the next bed corner to try once more, I yelled "NO GO!" and shook the can of pennies again. Goober's leg dropped, and this time he eyed me with suspicion. As I expected, Goober then tottered all the way around to the other side of the bed for a third attempt, and when I screeched "NO GO!" and shook the can of pennies, he looked at me like, "What is this guy's problem?" And when he headed for the fourth corner, all I had to do was raise the can of pennies before he dropped his leg, sat down, and looked up at me with eyes that said, "We obviously need to talk."

The next morning, I gladly canceled all appointments and spent the entire day with Goober tethered to me. Every single time he sniffed, circled, or so much as looked at a vertical object, I shook and screamed, and within forty-eight hours,

Goober associated marking in the house with me throwing tantrums or doing a bad mambo, and quit.

If you can't be right next to your dog for two days, confine him to a small area and watch him for the first few minutes, during which he will probably do most of his marking. When he starts to lift his leg, shake the can of pennies and yell. Later, when you get home and let him out, watch him as closely as possible. Consistency is the most important factor here, and while it may take a few weeks to break the habit, he *will* eventually cave. Always follow up good behavior with some loving and praise.

Submissive Urination

There—I used the word.

Had to, because this is a big one at Stray Rescue, where many of our volunteers and foster parents take on dogs who've been abused. We can't say "submissive peepee" or "submissive number-one" any more than we can say "submissive see-a-man-about-a-horse" and sound like we know what we're talking about.

I did try once, though. A guy called about a dog he'd adopted from us who did the deed every time he came home from work. He was a carpenter, and when he asked, "Man, why the hell does she piss every time she sees me?" I heard

the angry alpha male well up in his voice and knew right away
what the problem was.

"She's taking a leak submissively, man," I said, trying to use
language I thought he'd identify with—trying, in other words,
to sound like one of the guys.

"Huh?"

"You know, man, submissively whizzing, submissively
hosing things down?"

"Huh?"

"Okay, let's say there's a group of guys in a bar and one guy
says to another, 'Your wife is so fat that when she walks past
a window, we lose four days of sunlight,' and everyone laughs
except the guy with the fat wife, who doesn't understand it's
a joke, and he's so afraid he's about to get beat up for having a
fat wife, he squats down and pisses on the floor to show that
he's no threat."

Silence on the other end.

"See, the man with the fat wife is showing submissiveness.
He doesn't *stand up* and piss on a bar stool; he *squats down*
and pisses on the floor."

More silence.

"He's telling the other guy, 'I'm just a nobody. I'm no threat
to your status in this bar, so please don't beat me up.' "

Still more silence.

"Hello?"

"Man . . . what in the *hell* are you talking about?"

What I tried and apparently failed to communicate is that submissive urination is a problem much like territory marking in that it's an instinctual issue for dogs—a way of saying something without using words.

In a wolf pack, there are rules that members must follow in order to keep the pack intact and working. In a way, a wolf pack symbolizes a Hobbesian dictatorship, where all members of a group submit to the leader, no questions asked, because no matter how bad the leader is, *someone* has to lead, just like in politics. Wolves, like all pack animals, are afraid of being alone, because a solitary life is nasty, brutish, and very, very short, so a wolf—and its genetically challenged cousin, the dog—will do whatever it takes to remain a member of the group, including acting the fool, i.e., squatting and urinating in the leader's presence, which makes the leader feel better about himself and less inclined to beat anyone up.

So the carpenter's dog who saw a man about a horse every time he walked in the door was simply telling him: I acknowledge that you are and always will be the leader. I am no threat. I want to remain part of this pack. *Please*.

Dogs who are naturally timid or anxious and those who've been abused or yelled at a lot are the ones most likely to urinate in submission. If she squats and pees whenever someone approaches her, or walks in the door and greets her, or scolds her in any way—and if she then rolls over and exposes her belly or crouches low to the ground—she's trying to communicate her passivity, her lack of ego, her total and unquestionable devotion to you, the leader of the pack.

While you *do* want to be leader of the pack, you don't need the pack's sole citizen reminding you every time you walk in the door.

- Never *ever* scold or punish her when she urinates in submission. You'll only confuse the hell out of her, because she won't make the connection. Consequently, she'll submissively urinate even more to make up for whatever it was that made you mad, even though she doesn't know what that was.

- When you walk in the door, don't make a big deal about greeting her. Pretend she's not there. Don't even look at her.

- A few minutes after you enter, greet her quietly by bending down and petting her on her side or under her chin. Don't make direct eye contact and don't pet her on top of the head. In fact, don't do anything that in any way resembles a dominant wolf: Don't rush toward her when you greet her (dominant wolves rush at submissive wolves before they attack); don't stand over her (dominant wolves try to stand "over" submissive wolves); and, don't pee on any vertical surface to mark territory.

When I talked with the carpenter, I figured he might have a hard time acting non-dominant, so I suggested he have a treat ready every time he walked in the door. If you can condition your dog to expect a treat whenever you greet each other, she'll quickly see you as a benevolent dictator instead of a jerk she has no choice but to live with.

The trick is to build her confidence by deflating your own. (For more on this, see chapter 11.)

Anxiety: When You Leave

If your dog sees a man about a horse whenever you leave the house, she's not doing it out of spite (probably not, anyway). This is an anxiety issue, which needs special attention (see chapter 10).

Cleaning Up

I've tried just about every commercially available odor destroyer on the market, and while many of them work well, they get expensive if you have a leaky dog, or, as in my case, *many* leaky dogs.

Back when I house-trained Bonnie's thirteen puppies, for instance (remember now, this is before Stray Rescue existed and before I turned into Dr. Doolittle and got to appear on national TV and attend cool Hollywood benefits because I knew what I was doing), I panicked and all but gave my bank account and social security numbers to the pet-store employees in exchange for something, *anything* to get rid of the smell. I bought magic formulas, miracle formulas, and formulas with guaranteed talismanic abilities, including an alchemistic solution, a seven-step solution, and a solution that "exorcised" evil spirits and smells. I bought pet perfume, odor-eating candles, and Air Wick by the case.

As I neared bankruptcy, my mom suggested vinegar, to which I rolled my eyes the way one does when one's mother suggests a remedy from the eighteenth century.

"It's cheap," she said.

"Okay, Mom."

"It works on windows too."

I never would have tried vinegar had I not rushed home one day to make dinner for incoming guests and found the thirteen teenybopper beasties, who had escaped from the basement, seeing men about horses throughout my house. Since I was out of my Oxi-Magic Pee Be Gone and didn't have time to go to the store, I grabbed a bottle of balsamic/raspberry vinegar and doused everything.

And . . . it worked. Once it dried, the vinegar smell disappeared and took the smell of beastie pee along with it. Amazed and happy, I also used it on my garden salad that night.

CHAPTER EIGHT

Dogs Who Lick Baby Snot

Help, Randy!

   We adopted a dog from you about eight years ago when she was four. She's been great for the most part, but we had a baby about six months ago and it's been chaos ever since. Buffy knocks over the Diaper Genie and pulls out dirty diapers. Another problem is her licking. After feeding the baby, or when the baby is sitting in her pumpkin seat, Buffy will not leave her alone. She wants to lick her constantly. I find it disgusting and unsanitary. She is not aggressive, but we can no longer control her, and I'm at my wits' end. I feel like I have to constantly watch her, and she's feeling like more work than our baby.

   Thanks,
   Frazzled

Dear Frazzled,
    Dare I say, "Buffy's mouth is prob-
ably more sanitary than anything *you*
wipe your baby's face with" and get away
with it?
    All the best,
    Randy

"Diaper Genie" and "pumpkin seat" are extremely foreign words to me, and when I called one of my volunteers for definitions—a woman named Sandy with small kids who screech in the background like wild animals in trees—she told me, between several threats to the heirs, that, "Duh—a Diaper Genie is a little man who lives in a bottle whose sole purpose in life is soil management."

"Huh?"

"Yeah, and a pumpkin seat is . . . hang on a minute . . . *Be QUIET while Mommy's on the phone* . . . a pumpkin seat is a giant magic squash that you put kids in when they won't be quiet, which flies away to a magic planet. Hang on a minute . . . *I SAID, be QUIET* . . . and doesn't come back until you get off the phone."

I guess I should have gotten the hint and called her back in eighteen years, but instead I asked if I could come by and talk to her about how she coped with three rescued dogs and two kids in one house.

"Sure," she said, and then cupped her hand over the receiver so that all I heard was a few muffled, unprintable threats, "but come armed."

I grabbed my can of pennies and headed for the door.

Have I pointed out that I do not have human children? The last time the subject came up was when my partner at the time, Jean Claude the Annoying, suggested we adopt a baby from China or Costa Rica. He made a big production of it: rosemary martinis before dinner; pinot noir with watercress-stuffed chicken for dinner; and warmed Grand Marnier with coffee and lemon wedges after dinner. I was thoroughly enjoying a cigarette and second snifter of Grand Marnier when he popped the question, and after clarifying that he meant a bipedal hominid as opposed to a puppy, I downed the rest of the Grand Marnier and lit another cigarette from the burning stub of the first.

At first, I argued about the financial costs associated with raising a kid (he'd get a second job), followed with time commitments (he'd quit his second job), and after exhausting a move to the suburbs ("an adventure"), making friends with Republican neighbors ("multicultural expansion"), and the purchase of a Volvo ("one small sacrifice"), I finally argued the obvious.

"But *who* would actually take care of it?"

"The Volvo?"

"The heir."

To which he had no response.

So, when I arrived at Sandy's house with the can of dependable pennies, I rang the doorbell with the knowledge that I had no knowledge about how one copes with both dogs and children in the same house. My mission of going straight to the source for answers, however, turned south the minute she opened the door.

Dogs bayed, children howled, somewhere a television blared. The chaos overwhelmed me, and as I stepped in and tried in vain to get my bearings, a phone rang in another room. Sandy handed me one of the midgets and then disappeared.

The midget smelled like a skunk. I held him/her out in front of me at arm's length, and the second he/she got a good look at me, he/she screamed. This got the dogs all excited about a possible game of Grab Dangling Sock from Baby's Foot, and as they danced in circles under his/her wildly flailing legs, I danced in circles in the opposite direction, engrossed in my own game of Keep Feet Attached to Baby Until Mother Returns.

I ran out of breath before the inevitable. The sock was lost to Mitzy, a small black-and-white street dog we'd rescued several years before, and as she raced around the room with her new prize, I couldn't help but compare the before and after.

My assistant Jenn and I had found Mitzy huddled under a trailer at an abandoned worksite, shaking from cold and starvation. Her rescue should have been an easy one. She was small for a street dog, too weak to run and too scared to bite, but as we tried pulling her out from under the trailer, she dug her nails into the frozen ground and held on with the stubbornness of a pit bull.

"Come on, sweetie—no one's going to hurt you."

With a pit bull, you can grab their dense muscles with the strength of a vise, but this little thing was so thin and frail, I worried I'd break every bone in her body if I pulled too hard.

"No one's going to hurt you. I promise."

Her tenacity surprised me. Usually the small dogs we rescued were victims of abuse, and while their fear of more pain might cause them to run, if cornered, their only defense was no defense, so they usually cowered submissively in acknowledgment of their size. This little girl, though, directed every ounce of strength left in her body to her clawing nails, and she clung with courage to her spot. Even the hot-dog lure, which no starving dog can resist, didn't work.

In the end, we resorted to using a noose, and as we pulled her out, thrashing against its hold, the reason for her fight appeared: two dead, frozen puppies underneath her, which she had tried in vain to keep warm.

Her whimpers for them, which turned to gut-wrenching yelps the farther we walked away, haunted me for weeks.

So, I let her keep the sock.

As the other two dogs chased Mitzy across the couch, under the coffee table, and over the chairs, Baby wailed so hard in my outstretched arms that snot bubbled and spewed from his/her nose like lava from a hyperactive volcano. Meanwhile, out of nowhere, Sandy's other child entered the room in a round baby-walker thing, and when, lost in their frenzy, the dogs bumped into it one by one, the walker and its inhabitant spun in circles with the centrifugal force of a carnival ride.

With the dogs out of control and both children now screaming, I decided the best thing to do was leave. I maneuvered Baby through the dogs to the couch and plopped him/her down.

"SIT."

Then I uprighted the overturned baby-walker thing.

"STAY."

Then I grabbed the sock from the mouth of one of the bigger dogs and gave it back to Mitzy.

Then I headed for the door.

This letter of advice might have ended abruptly here with "Don't have children," had I not seen the can of pennies, which must have dropped out of my hands during the first few horrifying minutes of my arrival.

I use the can of pennies—about twenty does the trick—as part of my EZ dog-training system for overall rude and/or rowdy behavior.

The Can of Pennies System:

- If the dog barks too much, shake the can of pennies and he'll stop.
- If the dog stares at you while you eat, shake the can of pennies, and he'll go stare at someone else.
- If the dog jumps up on you every time you walk through the door, shake the can of pennies, and he'll run and hide instead.

I keep about twelve cans of pennies in strategic locations throughout my house, and if I even *reach* for one, halos appear above my dogs' heads and they all but bow in my presence.

Slowly, to increase the surprise, I bent down and picked up the can of pennies at Sandy's door. Then I turned and faced the rioters, which now included Mitzy and another dog playing tug-of-war with Baby's sock on top of the coffee table, Baby on the couch howling as another dog licked snot off his/her face, and the child in the baby-walker thing spinning in circles and shrieking with outstretched arms for his/her mother.

With the stony calm of Lady Liberty, I raised the can of pennies above my head, inhaled deeply, and then . . . I shook it.

Every head in the room jerked my way, each with dropped jaws, widened eyes, and its own version of WHAT-IN-THE-HELL-WAS-*THAT?* plastered across its face.

And just like that, complete silence.

From that point on, if one of the heirs scowled or squeaked, or if one of the dogs even thought of resuming their little party, I shook the can of pennies and restored quiet so that by the time Sandy waltzed back into the room, all five members of the uprising sat in a row on the couch like shiny little trophies on a mantelpiece.

"Wow," Sandy said as she stared suspiciously, hands on hips, at the couch.

The only problem with supreme power, a.k.a. a can of twenty pennies, is that it doesn't work on sneaky behavior— the stuff that kids and dogs do when you aren't looking. It also doesn't work on psychological issues and can, in some cases, make them worse. Sandy claimed, for instance, that if you shook a can of pennies at your kid every time he/she wouldn't eat their broccoli, he/she would end up with an eating disorder.

"Could you spray the kid in the face with the water bottle instead?" I asked.

Spraying dogs with the water bottle is much like shaking a can of pennies in that it's an unpleasant experience they learn to associate with certain behaviors. It works particularly well with excessive barking and jumping on furniture, and if you have a dog who eats turds out of the litter box (see chapter 5), all you have to do is add a little lemon juice or Tabasco sauce and *voilà*—marinated turds they won't touch.

Which brings me back to the letter-writer's first complaint: *Buffy knocks over the Diaper Genie and pulls out dirty diapers.*

Try this: Keep a spray bottle of water mixed with lemon juice and Tabasco sauce next to the Diaper Genie (whatever that is), and each time the apprentice pooper delivers a load, squirt the diaper with your special little marinade, and I guarantee the dogs won't go near it more than once.

The squirt bottle (filled with plain water) is also good for when baby starts to crawl. One of the biggest complaints I get is that the dog steps on the baby once he/she is on all fours, and if you just yell, "Don't stomp the baby," and give the dog a squirt each time, he'll leave the new plaything alone. You wouldn't even have to leave the couch with this method.

Which brings me to the letter-writer's second complaint: *Another problem is her licking. After feeding the baby, or when the baby is sitting in her pumpkin seat, Buffy will not leave her alone. She wants to lick her constantly. I find it disgusting and unsanitary.*

Well, you got the kid in the first place by swapping a little spit . . . but I guess that's irrelevant at this point. I suppose spraying the baby's face with lemon juice and Tabasco sauce is off limits too . . .

Try this: Whenever Buffy tries to kiss the kid, shake the can of pennies. It gets no easier than that.

If, however, you're hell-bent on making this complicated, you can send Buffy to obedience class once a week. While I would have started planning this out well before the kid arrived, better late than never. An obedience class not only ensures that your dog is well behaved, but it also builds a strong foundation of socialization experience, because a dog who learns to handle himself in a crowded room filled with other dogs and people will also handle himself around the baby.

I've come to understand, though, via letters, e-mails, and phone messages, usually from moms who sound like Tony Soprano—"I don't have !@#!-ING time to take a !@#!-ING shower. I haven't had a !@#!-ING shower in *SIX !@#!-ING WEEKS* and you want me to take the !@#!-ING dog to an obedience class once a !@#!-ING week?!?"—that this suggestion may not be appropriate during your time of distress. (*Note to Self*: Send condolence cards to all new parents in future.)

So instead of leaving the house once a week without having had a shower in six, teach the dog to sit by placing a food treat on her nose. Then raise the treat over her head so that as her eyes follow it up, her back end drops to the floor. As soon as this happens, give her the treat. Whenever the dog wants anything—to be petted, fed, played with, let outside— she must sit first.

Next, spread a baby blanket on the floor and place a baby doll or stuffed animal in the center. Bring your dog to the blanket and tell her to sit, and when she does, reward her with a treat. Eventually, she will learn that when she approaches the blanket, she's to sit near the edge no matter how interesting the object on it may be.

This approach obviously works better if you use it *before* the stork delivers the little bundle of stress, so if you're in this lucky position, consider the following as well:

Get the dog used to baby items, including rattles, blankets, the nifty Diaper Genie, and the pumpkin-pie seat. In essence, desensitize the dog to anything associated with the baby, especially the nursery.

Start by keeping the nursery door closed more often, and always at night, and use the *sit* command before she can enter the room. Once she's allowed to enter the nursery—if at all— make her sit by both the crib and the changing table.

You also want to desensitize the dog to baby smells. Consider dusting the house with baby powder, and then borrow some unwashed baby blankets from a friend, which you then place on the floor. If the dog so much as sniffs the blanket, let alone tries to lie down on it, shake your can of pennies or give her a squirt with the water gun and redirect her to a more appropriate place.

Once in a great while, a new parent calls me and says the *family* dog growls at the *new* baby. I stress those two words, because the situation usually only occurs when this is a family's first baby and is nothing more than a temporary case of new-sibling jealousy.

Think about it: For thousands of years, we've selectively bred as much of the wolf out of the dog as we can, which means we're basically left with a hairy two-year-old kid who makes a lot of noise and licks his own butt. Like a toddler, he depends on us for everything. He can't hunt, he can't problem-solve, he can't imagine any world besides his own, so when you—his parent—bring home *someone else*, routines, affections, and everything else and then some changes.

He is, in effect, confused.

So make it easy for him to understand. Whenever you hold the baby, reward the dog; whenever you feed the baby, feed the dog; whenever you change the baby's diaper, give the dog a treat. If you reward your dog every time he comes near the baby (and sits on command), it won't be long before the baby becomes your dog's favorite person, besides you.

Finally, *never* punish the dog for growling, because that only teaches him not to warn before biting. Remember, growling is not a bad thing—it's the only way your dog has of warning your child that he/she is too close, too smelly, or too annoying.

As a last resort, you can always put the baby in a plastic bubble (which would be my choice, personally). It would make for great conversation when you have company and could be great exercise for the baby.

Quick Fix-4

Dumping Excuse: "The dog sheds too much."

Quick Fix: Go to your closet and pull out that nifty little gadget called a "vacuum cleaner."

CHAPTER NINE

Bullies with an Attitude

Dear Randy,

You talked with my wife, Darla, a couple of weeks ago about Copper, a dog we adopted from Stray Rescue. Please contact us as soon as possible to make arrangements for her to be returned to your organization.

Copper is a very dominant alpha female. Sometimes it's either her way or no way. We have had her for about a year and a half. We think she is about three or four years old.

There were some times in the past where she tried to enforce her dominance over me to the point of not allowing me to get into my side of the bed at night. She also refuses to let us cut her nails to the point of snapping at Darla. With all the dogs we have ever had, we have always brushed them and clipped their nails with no problems.

We are not interested in a behavioral analysis. As I stated above, I appeal to you to please take her back. Perhaps she would be better off on a

farm or something like that, but at any
rate, I will no longer put up with these
incidents.

Sorry, Randy; we tried to make it
work out, but the situation has gone
beyond what we think is a reasonable
attempt to straighten her out.

Sincerely,
The Dumps

Dear Mr. Dump,

First: Please advise me where this
magical "farm" is located—the one that
you and every other dog dumper believe
exists. I've never found it, and believe
me, I've looked.

Second: What does Copper's dominance
issues have to do with a farm anyway?
Can Copper milk cows and feed the chick-
ens?

Third: (Grab a stiff drink, because
this will hurt.) Unbeknownst to you, I
talked to your wife on the phone, and
she really doesn't want to give Copper
up. In fact, she called me looking for
"secret advice," and when I asked her
why it needed to be secret, she told
me you "made all the decisions in the
household" and would be "furious" if you
knew she'd called me. I won't damage
your ego any further by telling you what
advice I gave her . . .

Sincerely,
Randy Grim

(*Note to Reader*: I'm not betraying
Mrs. Dump's confidence by revealing her
phone call, because she followed my advice and dumped Mr. Dump not long after
this incident.)

While aggression in dogs takes several forms, if their behavior involves any of the following, I'd bet my secret stash of Reese's Peanut Butter Cups that it's dominance aggression:

- She growls at you when you get near her food bowl, take a toy away from her, or try to get into bed when she's already there.
- She acts aggressively toward some family members and not others.
- She insists on being petted sometimes and growls when you do it at other times (especially when she's resting).

It's easy to confuse dominance aggression with fear aggression (see chapter 10), but if a dog growls at you from a crouched position with her eyes averted, then it's fear, and if she growls while in an upright position, staring at you with a look that says, "You are a quarter-pounder," then it's dominance.

Whenever a person contacts me about a dominant-aggressive dog, I first run them through Randy's Power-Freak Personality Disorder Test, because many people who have dominance issues with their dogs also have dominance issues with their people. Dr. Gupta says they have *asymmetrical dyadic relationships*, which sounds like they worship Satan, because they try to control others by limiting choices, and using physical or psychological abuse, but I just call them people who shouldn't have dogs. (*Note to Self*: Consider replacing the MEAN PEOPLE SUCK bumper sticker on my van with ASYMMETRICAL DYADIC PEOPLE SUCK.) So Part I of my test consists of starting a few sentences and then . . . pausing.

"So you're calling about . . ."

". . . Copper."

"You said in your e-mail that Copper growls when you get into . . ."

". . . bed."

"And she doesn't like her toenails . . ."

". . . trimmed."

If they finish the sentence for me, then I move on to Part II, which I designed with the following cleverly camouflaged questions:

1) Do you reprimand your wife when she buys the wrong toothpaste?
2) Do you think the world would be a better place if you ran it?
3) Do you yearn to wear a crown?
4) Do you identify with your inner ape?

If they answer "Well . . . yeah," as if they were stupid questions, then I move on to Part III, which is asking them what their address is, and what time I should pick up the dog.

Usually, and unfortunately, the reason dominance-aggression problems arise between dogs and their people is that the people don't know how to lead. All too often, I receive calls and e-mails laced with phrases including "I did an alpha roll," "I stared him down," and "I made him submit," but in most cases the e-mails end with, "and he bit me anyway." So, let's get one thing out of the way right now: DO NOT EVER try to dominate an aggressive dog physically unless you like visiting emergency rooms. DO NOT stare him down. DO NOT attempt the so-called alpha roll, which I explain below. DO NOT yell, hit, or challenge him in any way, because he will eventually take your arm off in an attempt to save the family.

Yes, in an attempt to *save the family*.

Here's what's going on: Researchers who studied wolves years ago thought packs organized themselves according to a hierarchy of physical power, with the strongest male and female dominating the others with force. They based this theory on what they thought they saw: alpha males and females forcing subordinates to grovel by flipping them to the ground and then staring them into submission as if they were in a WWF wrestling match. They called it the "alpha roll," not related to the popular egg roll, and it eventually became a trendy dog-training technique in which people were told, among other things, to grab an aggressive dog by the neck, force it down onto its back, and then hold the sides of his cheeks while staring directly into his eyes. Advocates of the alpha roll and other physical techniques (including—I'm not kidding—hanging dogs from trees and choking them nearly to death) thought that if wolves used force to control the pack, people should too.

The problem—what I call The Great Misconception Meant to Make Randy's Life Difficult—is that the early wolf researchers got it WRONG, all WRONG, and, in fact, SO WRONG, that this trendy little dog-training technique resulted in trendy little stitches for many sorry people. You wouldn't believe how many power freaks glommed onto the alpha-roll theory and how many of their dogs I re-rescued as a result.

What researchers thought they were seeing—an alpha wolf grabbing a subordinate and flipping it to the ground—was actually the subordinate wolf *offering* his muzzle to the leader who then placed his own muzzle *gently* over it. The subordinate then *voluntarily* rolled to the ground. Reread the italicized words in the last sentence, because they're important to remember when dealing with an aggressive dog. It is more like Wolf Theater and acting. The leader wolf doesn't use force; the subordinate wolf volunteers submission (as in, willingly). The only time, and I mean the *only time* a wolf uses force against another wolf is when he wants to kill it, literally, and as contemporary wolf researcher David L. Mech wrote in his paper, "Alpha Status, Dominance, and Division of Labor in

Wolf Packs," "Dominance contests with other wolves are rare, if they exist at all."

This takes us back to why an aggressive dog is often just trying to save his family. According to Dr. Mech and others who've actually lived with wolves, the alpha male and female do not lead as pistol-carrying tyrants who use force to control the pack, but rather as parents who use diplomacy to control who sits where at dinnertime. A wolf pack is, in fact, a family unit usually consisting of the parents, their pups of various ages from various litters, and an outsider or two allowed in from other packs to keep things copacetic. There's no mysterious, primal, hierarchical structure here; a wolf pack is simply a wolf family, and the alpha male and female are Mom and Dad— pretty basic *Brady Bunch* logic here.

As such, Mom and Dad rule, and any displays of "dominance" are really just Mom and Dad making sure everyone stays safe and gets fed. When the pack brings down prey, for example, Mom and Dad eat first—not because they need to display their power, as previously thought, but to keep themselves strong enough to take care of the kids (why I eat first at home with my "kids"). It's the same principle behind putting the air mask over your own face before Junior's when the plane goes down. They in turn decide who eats next. If times are good—and for wolves, this would be when large prey like moose are taken down—everyone eats at the same time. If times are bad and the prey is small, Mom and Dad "ration" by feeding the youngest pups first and allotting the older siblings only what's left. "Thus," Mech writes, "the most practical effect of social dominance is to allow the dominant individual the choice of to whom to allot food." Simple as that: It's all about groceries.

The only fighting or jostling for dominance in a wolf family takes place among the pups, who establish future alphas while they're little, before they can inflict any real harm on each other. Once pups decide potential alpha-ness, it's pretty much set in stone for the rest of their lives. That way, when Mom or Dad get older, or die, the successor has already been chosen and can step peacefully into place.

Mom and Dad, therefore, "rule" with calm, inherent authority, because they have nothing to prove. As parents, they are leaders in the purest sense of the word, because their goal has nothing to do with self-interest but with the safety of the family as a whole. They don't bare their teeth or roll subordinates to the ground or in any way strut their stuff to display their strength, because as parents, as true leaders, they don't *need* to.

And neither do you.

If you bring a new dog into your family and he acts aggressively toward you, it's because he doesn't understand who's leading the pack. You, apparently, aren't, so for him it's like entering a pack of insecure, squabbling pups, trying to determine future alpha-ness. If even one leadership chromosome inhabits his body, he'll step in to fill the void, because in every functional family, *someone* has to take charge.

Let me regurgitate: Your new dog, the biological equivalent of a wolf pup, enters your home expecting to find the functional fairy-tale family, complete with calm, dignified parental leaders and kids who adore and obey them. But if he possesses any dominant tendencies and finds no leadership— the leadership that should be there, that must be there if his new pack is to survive—he'll automatically assume that role so the pack *does* survive. He thinks he is helping restore order to the dysfunctional clan.

In other words, when your dominant-aggressive dog growls or bites, he is not challenging your authority; he's already assumed leadership and is reprimanding *you* for challenging *his*.

Unfortunately, and in large part because of The Great Misconception Meant to Make Randy's Life Difficult, dominance aggression in dogs usually plays out as follows:

Scene I: Mr. Dump decides the family should have a dog and assigns Mrs. Dump the task of finding several candidates from which he can choose. Mr. Dump chooses Copper, a seemingly docile, well-behaved female.

Scene II: Copper enters her new pack expecting Mr. and Mrs. Dump to act like rational and mature alphas, only Mr. Dump acts like an adolescent beta (physically aggressive, stomps around yelling a lot, proves his point ad nauseam), and Mrs. Dump acts like a submissive omega (physically passive, lavishes undue affection, provides unlimited food in the bowl). Copper assumes the alphas were killed by musk oxen while out hunting.

Scene III: Copper decides she must save this dysfunctional pack from certain extinction, so she steps up and fills the leadership vacancy. She doesn't want to, but the only other candidate is the parakeet, and he's behind bars.

Scene IV: While Mrs. Dump seems to understand her position as lowest in the pack, Mr. Dump doesn't understand his. He indirectly challenges Copper's authority on a regular basis—he growls, he raises his hackles, he tries to clip her toenails—and while she uses strict but fair reprimands to nip things in the bud (quite literally), he just doesn't get it.

Scene V: Mr. Dump goes too far one day and grabs Copper by the throat, throws her to the ground, and pushes his face up into hers. It is a direct challenge, and he means to kill her.

Copper responds accordingly.

Finale: Mr. Dump writes a "Dear Randy" letter.

Almost any dog, no matter how dominant, will resign his leadership post if a better leader surfaces. Remember, dogs are mentally equivalent to wolf pups, and if you act like their parent—like a true leader who controls the resources without using force—they will follow you gladly. Consider which boss you'd throw a lifeline to if necessary: the short-tempered, highly stressed bully who uses threats of demotions and firings based on compliance, or the even-tempered, calm-headed boss who promises promotions based on merit.

While we've spent the last billion paragraphs setting up the solution, which was necessary, the solution itself is the easiest in the entire book to accomplish. It's so easy, in fact, that you might feel a little cheated when you find out that all you have to do is . . .

. . . teach the dog to sit.

The collective "Huh?" that just escaped the lips of the audience was expected, so never fear, Randy is here, with an explanation almost as simple as the solution itself: Since leaders control the resources, *you* must control the resources.

If you control the resources, you are by definition the alpha, and the dog's dominance aggression disappears.

What are the resources? The things your dog wants (food, toys, and access to the yard).

How do you control the resources? Teach him to sit before he gets them.

Before the dog gets food, he sits. Before he goes outside, he sits. Before you pet him, play with him, or even glance in his direction, he sits. Every time. For every resource.

Three important distinctions need to be made at this point. One is that you are not *forcing* your dog to sit; you are *teaching* him to sit to get what he wants. If he doesn't sit when you ask him, he doesn't get access to the goods. It's as simple as that. You don't yell at him or coerce him to sit. He sits, period. If he doesn't sit the first time you ask him, you walk away and he doesn't get what he wants. There's no emotion involved whatsoever, which is important, because alphas don't humor anybody in any way. (Just had a flashback to Sister Agnes; maybe she was a werewolf.)

The second distinction is that leaders initiate and followers react. This is a well-worn, classic concept, but as the alpha, you must initiate access to resources rather than your dog. So, for instance, if you sit on your couch and the dog comes up to you looking for attention and you pet him, he initiated and you reacted. If you sit on the couch and the dog comes up to you looking for attention and you ask him to sit, he sits, and then you pet him, guess what? He still initiated and you still reacted. If, however, you sit on the couch, the dogs seeks attention, you completely ignore him until he walks away, and *then* you ask him to sit, he sits, and you pet him, *you* have initiated and *he* has reacted.

The third distinction is that this is not a power struggle you are required to win every time. Case in point: You bring a new, adult dog into your life who growls if you get too close to him while he's eating. This isn't a fight worth fighting, believe me, and it doesn't make sense to try. Even omega wolves growl at alphas if they invade eating space. The important point is that the alpha gave the food in the first place. The alpha controlled the resource from the start. If it weren't for the alpha, the omega wouldn't be eating. So if your dog is protective of his food, leave him alone while he's eating, but *make sure he sits before you give him the food*. In time you can desensitize his food aggression by feeding him out of your hand. I recommend to everyone who has a puppy that you feed the animal from your hands, and pet, touch, and talk while the li'l guy is eating, for this will save you from writing me in a year with a stitched-up finger.

Okay, let's say you've just brought home your new pack member, a cute, little, yellow dog named Omelet, and for a week or two, he's a great dog: He's house-trained, he fetches, and he loves your attention. You in turn are a great parent: You buy a wicker basket for his toys, so he can play with them whenever he wants; you leave a full bowl of dry food out so he can eat when he's hungry; and, you give him comfy spaces on your couch and bed and pet him whenever he wants, so he feels loved.

But then one day, you try to take Omelet's stuffed purple octopus away, and he growls and maybe even snaps quickly in your direction. Depending on your personality, either you yank your hand back and say, "I'm sorry," or you grab the stuffed octopus out of his mouth and yell, "BAD OMELET!"— both normal reactions based on fear, but both inappropriate, because they show Omelet your loss of emotional control.

Then Omelet starts growling whenever you walk within twelve feet of *his* wicker basket. He starts growling when you get near *his* food bowl. Then Omelet starts growling when you give him a bath or clip his nails, because you're invading *his* personal space.

And then one night, Omelet jumps in *his* bed, but when you follow, he growls. Again, depending on your personality, either you sneak a pillow off the bed and sleep on the floor, or you threaten him with the pillow and eternal damnation. When Omelet reacts by snapping the air in your direction, you fall completely off your rocker and grab him by the throat, drag him onto the floor, hold him down, and hiss something alpha-esque, like *"I am the boss,"* while staring him directly in the eyes, and Omelet, who thinks you're threatening *his* life, defends himself. (All very reminiscent of my last relationship; which, my editor is quick to point out, is beside the point.)

Now, before I tell you what an idiot you were, I must clarify that many dogs, especially timid ones, will thrive on love and affection. As long as they show no dominance aggression toward you, love away. If, however, they are like Omelet and *do* have dominance tendencies, then you've basically handed them the resources and the leadership perks that go with them. You gave him endless toys, unlimited food, and unconditional access to your attention, all with no strings attached, which Omelet read as, "We're idiots. Please lead us."

So, you made some mistakes. Here's how you fix them:

1) **Stage the Coup**

   Have someone take Omelet for a walk. While he's gone, throw away the wicker basket, hide all of his toys on the top shelf of the hall closet, and pick up his food bowl and hide that too.

2) **Commence the Transition**

   When Omelet gets home, ignore him. Don't greet him at the door and don't pet him for the rest of the day. He'll probably pace around looking for his stuff, and when he doesn't find it, he'll whine and demand your attention. Pretend he's not there. Don't feed him, and don't give him his toys. When he needs to go out, have him sit first, give him one small treat—don't say "Good boy" or in any way praise him—and then let him out. That night, do not let him in the bedroom.

3) Take Control of the Resources

From this point forward, act aloof around Omelet and have him sit before you give him anything, including your attention. Since you gave him no access to food the day before, he'll be hungry, so start with a simple request to sit while you're holding out a treat. When he sits, give him the treat but don't say anything to him. Act aloof. Now, take out his leash and have him sit before you open the door. If he doesn't sit, say nothing, and show no emotion; just walk away and try again five minutes later. Eventually, he'll get the idea and sit. When it's time to eat, take out the food bowl, put food in it, and then ask him to sit. If he doesn't sit, walk away and try again later, though he probably will, because he's pretty hungry by now. By the time you're ready to give him a toy, he should know the drill. It's your toy now, not his, and if he wants to play, he has to request permission by sitting when you ask.

Then, for the rest of the day—and for the rest of his life—repeat these actions before you give him anything.

Happy Endings for No-Win Situations

- Never take the food bowl away from him while he's eating. Once he sits and you reward him with food, it's his.
- Don't let him sleep on your bed at night—period. This helps avoid any misunderstanding about who's boss.
- Don't pit yourself against your dog with weapons such as nail clippers or running bath water. Why do you think God created grooming shops anyway? Let the groomer be the bad guy and you the hero when you pick him up, all nice and clean.

CHAPTER TEN

Cowardly Lions

Phone message #1: Morning, Randy, it's Jenn. Uh, someone chained a little dog wearing a diaper to the shelter door last night. There's a note that says, "Please take care of our Splinter. We love him, but he bites and pittles in the house, and we don't know what else to do with him." Call me back.

Phone message #2: Hello. We need a guest speaker for our conference. We are trying to locate Randy Grim.

Phone message #3: Randy, Jenn again. The little dog, Splinter, seems scared to death, so I'm going to have one of the volunteers take him for a walk until you call back . . .

Phone message #4: Hi, Randy. This is Dr. Gupta's office. We received a call from your pharmacy and instructed them not to refill your prescriptions until you make *and keep* your next appointment.

Phone message #5: This is Books-R-Us. Your order for *Reducing Anxiety through Hypnosis* has arrived.

Phone message #6: Randy, it's Jenn again. Splinter just bit one of the volunteers and we're on our way to the emergency room. Where are you? Why aren't you answering your phone? Call me back.

Dear Readers, someone hand me a noose, please.

Don't worry—I'd never use it, because along with aeronausiphobia (the fear of vomiting on airplanes), taeniophobia (the fear of tapeworms), triskaidekaphobia (the fear of the number 13), pupaphobia (the fear of puppets), and medomalacuphobia (which is too embarrassing to define here), I have also been diagnosed with thanatophobia (the fear of death), and something that hasn't been named yet, as far as Dr. Gupta knows—the fear of dying and not being found for several weeks and totally grossing out whoever finds me—which he thinks is a self-image issue rather than a phobia.

Anyway, the point is that I understand fear, and I understand why dogs like Splinter with fear aggression bite people. I fantasize about it all the time. The big problem is that it's hard to distinguish fear aggression from dominance aggression, which we treat very differently, so here are some visual clues that indicate fear versus dominance when she lashes out at you:

- He lowers or completely tucks his tail (dominant dogs raise their tails);
- he pulls his ears back horizontally (dominant dogs raise their ears);
- he looks away from you (dominant dogs stare you in the eye);
- he growls and snarls as a warning before he bites (dominant dogs usually don't bother with the warning); or
- his fur stands on end, and he salivates and/or urinates (sure signs of fear not displayed by dominant dogs).

Fearful dogs are usually either those who didn't socialize with people when they were puppies, who experienced abuse, or who have painful physical ailments. You can tell the difference this way: Unsocialized dogs are afraid of things in general, like all men and all children; abused dogs are afraid of specific things, such as belts or raised hands; and dogs with pain are afraid of being touched.

It's a fight-flight-freeze thing (from this point forward called the F-Word Syndrome) that Dr. Gupta described as "an acute stress response involving an intense discharge of the locus ceruleus that activates the sympathetic division of the automatic nervous system," which I asked him to write down, because I also have Hippopotomonstrosesquippedaliophobia, which is a fear of long words.

According to Dr. Gupta, dogs, people, and most other animals on earth (including some unfortunate rats born in laboratories) respond to threats by challenging them, running away from them, or freezing in place in an attempt to hide from them (my preferred method)—all *appropriate* responses when triggered by long-winded physiological things going on in the nervous system, triggered themselves by *real* threats like charging grizzly bears. Those of us with F-Word Syndrome, however, respond in *inappropriate* ways to *imaginary* grizzly bears and end up in city pounds or on therapists' couches.

Believe me, fear is a powerful motivator—I'd rather build an entire lock-and-dam system with my bare hands than drive over a bridge—but before you turn your snarling, slinking, snapping dog in to authorities, remember that fear is also controllable.

Case in point: Splinter.

Splinter terrified me from the day I met him. All five pounds of him. Someone dumped him on Stray Rescue's doorstep in the middle of the night, and not only did he look scary—imagine a cross between a Brillo Pad and a dust mop—but he wore a diaper and made these weird hissing noises that I quickly learned (when I tried to remove his diaper) were warning snarls emitted before he bit. Under normal circumstances, a five-pound toy dog would be easy to adopt out from our shelter, even one that looked and sounded like a rat with emphysema, but Splinter was too much of a little (I have to spell this out to avoid censure by the editor) s-h-i-t to just hand over to anybody unless you really, really hated them.

So he comes to *my* house to live for a while.

From the start, Splinter intimidated everyone in the house, including me; Charley, the sixty-five-pound pit bull; Horsey, the hundred-pound chow/rottweiler mix; Hannah, the schizophrenic; and Satan the Cat. On his first day, Splinter sat in a corner of the kitchen and established a twelve-foot safety perimeter around himself, which if crossed, initiated a volley of hissed insults followed by rapid-fire lunges and snaps that sent everyone running for cover. No one went into the kitchen that day, and despite my fear of drinking from the tap and eating fast food, the dogs, cats, and I guzzled bathroom water and dined on carry-out Thai while Splinter had food tossed into the kitchen followed by a quick door slam.

The next morning, in my usual un-caffeinated fog, I forgot about our houseguest and walked straight into the kitchen to make coffee as usual. Out of nowhere, this thing, this hissing, self-propelled dust mop that at first I mistook for an alien hedgehog, darted in my direction from the recesses of his universe. Need I tell you how painful it is to get from the floor to the countertop in just one leap? Meanwhile, my other dogs, my spineless, sissy, scaredy-cat companions, just stood at the threshold of the kitchen and stared up at me in sympathy.

"Wimps."

But it was from the vantage point of the countertop—upon which I spent a considerable amount of time crawling around on all fours, making coffee—that I devised my plan of attack.

It seemed pretty obvious that fear ruled Splinter's passions. Whenever we got near his safety zone, he turned his head away from us, raised his upper lip until his miniature yellow fangs showed, and then hissed his weenie version of a warning growl. When I approached him with bite gloves to take off his diaper, he flattened his ears horizontally and hissed, and when I used a broom to push his food bowl toward him from a safe distance, he raised his hackles and attacked the handle, intent on making it extinct. This told me he'd probably suffered abuse at some point in his life, because people's hands and objects freaked him out. In addition, he was a toy version of something or other, which meant he was probably reared in a puppy mill where he'd received no human attention or affection during the first critical weeks of his life. He was, in short, a homicidal, socially maladjusted, post-traumatic stress victim.

(Many of the dogs we work with at Stray Rescue are feral, meaning they grew up in the urban wilds and experienced little or no contact with human beings until we trapped them. These are special cases—equivalent to socializing wild wolf pups—and I've included information about them at the end of the chapter.)

Unlike Splinter, most family dogs with fear aggression only display one or two symptoms, such as snarling at strangers— especially men and children, or men who act like children— who try to pet them. If that's your case, consider yourself lucky, because dogs like Splinter with paranoid Napoleonic issues require all kinds of affection that's hard to give, because for several weeks, it's not reciprocated. Don't be dismayed; being super-nice to a creature who tries to bite you all the time teaches all kinds of useful life lessons, such as how to fake being nice to people you yourself can't stand. Thank you, Splinter.

Anyway, back to the countertop, where, in a cross-legged position and sipping my hard-won coffee, I mapped out Splinter's therapy: hot-dog counterconditioning, followed by several games of Circle People Who Owe You Money.

The first stage—hot-dog counterconditioning—teaches the dog a new way to respond to fear. The only hard part is getting from the countertop to the refrigerator to retrieve the hot dogs. If the refrigerator is aligned with the counter, it's simply a matter of stretching your leg out, latching onto the handle with your big toe, and pulling the door open. If your refrigerator sits across the room from the countertop, however, as mine does, you'll have to wait for the beast to retreat to his corner, and at just the right moment, rapidly jump off the counter and land on one foot while swinging the other foot up toward the top of the kitchen table. Once on the table, you can push the chairs out to form a path toward the fridge, and once you have the hot dogs in hand, you can fling one to the far end of the room (no dog can resist chasing a flying hot dog), which allows you time to escape.

To start the actual counterconditioning, teach your dog to sit and relax using cut-up hot dogs as a reward. I suggest hot dogs because it's important to use a treat that dogs can't resist, and hot dogs never fail me. What's even more important, though, is to remember not to reward the dog for sitting or staying, but for *relaxing*. You are trying to teach the dog to relax, not to sit, so he must believe the two go hand in hand if he's going to get his treat. Every time you ask him to sit, he must associate happiness and relaxation with doing the deed.

So, take the dog to a safe place that doesn't freak him out and ask him to sit. Then, wait for him to relax, and when he does, give him his treat. Repeat this over and over in different places, inside your house and out, and when he's mastered the art of chilling out, you're ready for the desensitizing game, Circle People Who Owe You Money.

There are many forms of fear in dogs, but since we're dealing with fear aggression toward people in this chapter, you'll have to find human volunteers to play this game. While you can use younger siblings, employees, or people who want you to like them, I suggest people who owe you money, because you can use them over and over again and not feel guilty, *and* they'll probably pay you back before the game is over.

I started by asking Splinter to sit at my feet while I called Jerry-the-friend-who-borrowed-$100-from-me and asked him if he could do me a small favor.

"Sure, of course—whatever you need," he said with saccharine enthusiasm.

"Great. Can you come to my front door, ring the bell, and then just stand there for a while?"

"Uh, sure, of course . . . uh, whatever you—"

"I need you to just stand there," I said. Splinter yawned at my feet, so I tossed him his hot dog. "No matter what."

"Uh . . ."

"No matter what."

Later, when Jerry rang the bell, I put a leash on Splinter, asked him to "sit" about nine feet away until he relaxed, and then I gave him a piece of hot dog. Slowly, I walked over to the door, telling Splinter to "stay," then I opened the door (I have no screen door), and when Jerry smiled and said, "Hi," Splinter stood up, his ears went sideways, his tail tucked, and he hissed his alien-rat-with-emphysema warning growl.

"What the hell is *that*?" Jerry said, but I slammed the door shut in his face.

"Sit," I told Splinter, who sat, but took a much longer time than usual to relax. When he finally did, I gave him his treat.

In the meantime, Jerry knocked softly. Splinter stood up, but I told him to "sit," and when he did, I gave him his treat and slowly opened the door.

"Hi," Jerry said again, but this time when Splinter stood up and went into his defensive posture, I told him to "sit."

"What . . . ?" Jerry asked.

"Shhh," I commanded as Splinter sat. "Just stand there and don't say anything."

It took a long time—maybe five minutes or more—but slowly Splinter's ears and tail relaxed, and the second they did, I gave him his treat. Remember, I was rewarding Splinter for sitting and relaxing in a stranger's presence—not just for sitting—and until he did, he received no treat.

Once Splinter had chilled at a distance of nine feet, I told Jerry to step inside the door.

"Is that thing going to bite me?"

"Don't say anything. Just step inside the door."

"But . . ."

"And whatever you do, don't *look* at him."

The point of Jerry not looking at Splinter was to reduce any perceived threat or challenge. It's really important to take this phase of the game s-l-o-w-l-y so as not to overwhelm the dog with fearful stimuli, and that includes the stranger looking, reaching, or talking to the dog. When I rescue dogs, I often wear sunglasses even on rainy days—not to be hip, but to reduce the dogs' anxiety levels. You are not trying to force him to like this stranger; you're forcing him to sit and relax when the stranger is at a far distance from him. The game then proceeds by strategically moving the person closer and closer to the dog while repeating the sit-and-relax exercise each time. Conversely, you could keep the dog on a leash and move the dog closer and closer to the person.

That's what I did with Splinter. After he relaxed with Jerry standing inside the door, I told the mooch to move to the center of the room and then walked the pooch on his leash in increasingly smaller circles around him. Whenever Splinter went extraterrestrial and Jerry asked if "that thing" was going to bite him, I asked Splinter to sit and relax, and then I asked Jerry for my $100.

You want to take this part very slowly for two reasons:

1) If you push a fearful dog into increasingly fearful situations without relaxing first, he'll never truly associate pleasure with being around people.

2) You want your volunteer to become more and more uncomfortable as the dog circles closer and closer, because, as was the case with Jerry, he'll suddenly remember he has a dentist appointment he has to get to, and, oh yeah, that he owes you money, which he'll pay immediately *with interest* as long as you never

ask a favor of him again. (This desired behavior is accomplished much sooner if your fearful dog is, say, a pit bull.)

So you'll have to find new volunteers, which is good, because you want your dog to associate relaxation and pleasure with as many strangers as possible. As the dog progresses, repeat the exercise with the volunteer sitting on the couch, moving through the living room, and then moving from the living room to the kitchen. Eventually, ask your volunteer to start tossing your dog his reward treat, and when you feel the time is right, have the volunteer offer the treat directly from his or her own hand. It may take days, or weeks, but sooner or later, he *will* accept the treat from the stranger's hand and you can declare a small victory.

You'll have to tailor the exercises to your dog's comfort level. Some get it right away and by the end of the first day of the game, sit on the volunteer's lap and beg for attention. Others take longer, sometimes much longer, and may in fact never really enjoy being in a stranger's presence. However, as long as they can relax in a stranger's shadow (and thus not attack), consider your efforts a success. So many fearful dogs at the shelter come around quickly once they are used to multiple loving people with food. They start to get it: People are not all bad.

Unfortunately, some dogs are so mentally screwed up from abuse and/or isolation, no amount of game-playing works on its own. In these cases, talk to your veterinarian about using antianxiety medication, such as clomipramine or fluoxetine, *in conjunction* with playing the game. These types of drugs calm the dog's nerves so well (without making them dopey), you could invite a 350-pound man dressed like Darth Vader into the house, and your dog may very well greet him warmly at the door. Gradually, as your dog learns to relax in the presence of even your weirdest friends, you can start reducing the amount of medication he takes, as well as your own pills.

Some Notes on Feral and Abandoned Dogs

There are degrees of "wildness" in feral and abandoned dogs, because some were dumped on the streets at early ages, while others were actually born out there. Those who were discarded early on may seem to be wild, but they actually do have memories of human contact, and they usually rehab more quickly. Every dog is different. You will notice some of them responding very quickly, while others can take many months.

- During the first twenty-four to forty-eight hours that your new dog is in your home, let him adjust to the new surroundings. You may notice pacing, whining, whimpering, even howling. He may not eliminate for up to three or four days, and he may not eat. This is normal.

- Feral dogs have a tendency to bolt because they're afraid. Use extreme caution when entering and exiting your house.

- Body language and tone of voice is crucial. Use slow, nonthreatening movements. Always use a calm monotone voice, avoiding a high baby voice or a stern voice, for these tones can actually frighten the dog more.

- Avoid direct eye contact. Crouching down low with your arm extended in a closed-hand fashion is a good way to begin a greeting.

- Spend time just being around your new dog. This is crucial, so read, do work, even watch TV in his presence as much as possible. The more human contact, the faster the rehab.

- Try not to force petting, as fear can lead to a bite. Read the dog's body language: If his ears go back, you stay back.

- Have plenty of great treats like hot dogs available. Gaining their trust includes proving you are the better hunter and thus nonthreatening.
- It may be a full month or longer before leash training can even begin; this means lots of cleanup. Do the cleanup slowly and calmly. Loud, strange noises can incite the dog to panic.
- When sufficient trust has been gained to use a leash, only walk the dog in the building, until it is certain he will not panic on the lead. A harness is preferable in the beginning, as it is nonthreatening.
- Habituating the feral to other dogs (especially well-adjusted dogs interacting with you) also helps them adjust quicker, allowing them to see how great humans can be.

CHAPTER ELEVEN

Allergy Season

Dear Randy,
    I became allergic to my dog . . .
    Sincerely,
    Every Third Person Returning Their
Dog

Dear Every Person Who Returns Their Dog
Because of Allergies,
    This excuse always makes me want
to hook you up to a lie detector test,
because how could so many people be
allergic to dogs? I do believe there *are*
people with allergies to their companion
animals, and my good friend Nicki is one
of those wheezing, runny-eyed people.
Here is what she said: "I am extremely allergic to dogs and cats and take
Flonase religiously (same time every
day). With it, I am able to live with
the greatest dog in the world, who likes
to sleep on my fiancé's lap. Note that it
loses some effectiveness when combined

```
with massive amounts of alcohol."
    So I surfed the Net and found too
many drugs to list, from Zyrtec to over-
the-counter Benadryl. The point being,
there is a better life through chemis-
try, so see a doctor, get tested, and
get the drugs that will work best for
you.
    Sincerely,
    Randy Grim
```

Here are some tips for other things you can do to make your home a more allergy-friendly one:

- Take your medicine. If you don't like to take pills, put it in a hot dog like you would for your dog.

- Be OCD and wash your hands after playing with the pooch.

- Once your shirt is covered in dog hair and looks more like an angora sweater than a T-shirt, change it.

- Go hardwood or tile; it's hip to have in your home, and won't collect allergens like carpet does.

- If you have carpet, make sure you clean it often. If you have children, put them to work and add vacuuming to their chore list.

- Use a hepa air cleaner; I have one in my bedroom for the dog smells alone, so it serves a double purpose.
- Change the air/heating filters often; 3M makes a great allergen-reducer filter.
- Take your dog to the groomer regularly, and that alone will cut down on allergens big-time.

(*Note to Self*: Talk to pharmaceutical companies about donating samples to all the shelters so we can include them in our adoption kits. That, or send us the money to hire a doctor to prescribe the allergy medicine and an FBI agent to administer the lie detector test.)

Quick Fix-5

Dumping excuse: "I didn't know how much time having a dog would require."
Quick Fix: Too bad. If you adopted him, live up to your responsibilities and make time.

CHAPTER TWELVE

Scaredy Cats

```
To: Randy Grim
From: Stray Rescue Volunteer
   Not sure it's working out with
Dodger. Still hides when people come
over and still pees when anyone pets
him. It's been several weeks now. May-
be he needs to be in quieter household
where there aren't so many other dogs.
```

```
To: Stray Rescue Volunteer
From: Randy Grim
   As you know, we rescued Dodger and
his brother from an abandoned house
where they were born and raised by their
stray mom. In technical terms, he is a
feral dog. And you need to be patient
with such dogs.
```

We named him Dodger for a reason: He dodges humans because they scare him, and when cornered, he sees a man about a horse on the floor, on your shoes, on himself, or worst of all, a foul back-end explosion in surrender. I identify with him completely (not the back-end explosion part) and would have fostered him myself except that my house is currently inundated with socially challenged dogs, including Dodger's brother, Bud, and if I take in any more, it will give the neighbors the ammunition they need to have my house raided by authorities and condemned, and trust me, I do not look good in stripes.

Because Dodger and Bud were feral dogs, we couldn't just keep them at the shelter and hope for the best. Truly wild dogs like them are the ultimate shy, overly submissive cases—their fear of humans is what kept them alive—so socializing them, or any shy dog, into the human pack requires pathological patience, because no matter how kind you are to them, no matter how many treats, hugs, or whispers of assurance you give them, they still act as if you're about to kill them. After a few days, you start to feel insulted—it's the ultimate rejection—and man's best friend thinks you are the bogeyman.

When Bud first came to my house, he'd never been on a leash, so I carried him in my arms from the Jeep to the door, because I didn't want to put any more stress on him than necessary. *I* thought I was being nice. *He* thought he was being carried away by the bogeyman to be eaten, and thus saw men about horses and covered me with back-end explosions the whole way.

When we got inside, my dogs swarmed around him for inspection. *They* thought that they'd found a new friend to play with. *He* thought he was about to be attacked en masse, so he tried to make himself invisible by flattening his ears, tucking his tail, crouching down as low as possible to the ground, and then slinking through their legs to escape.

The gang followed him to the kitchen where he crawled under the table. *They* thought he was leading them on a game of chase and pursued accordingly. *He* thought he was being cornered by predators and rolled on his back and stared at the wall—his way of begging them not to attack.

They thought, "Wimp," got bored, and eventually walked away. *He* thought, "I'm still alive," and stayed flattened to the floor under the table before scurrying to make his nest under my bed for the next three days. For those three days it was like having a prisoner sentenced to solitary confinement lurking under the mattress. At night I would slide his meals under the bed, and by morning the bowl would be pushed back out, empty. This also meant having to withstand putrid smells seeping out from beneath my prison cot of a bed. I moved to the guest bedroom with a bottle of Febreze.

It's all a matter of misinterpretation.

In the wolf world, where everyone understands each other, all of Bud's reactions make sense. From a very young age, wolf pups elicit regurgitated food from the adults by crouching down, tucking their tails, and licking the sides of the adult's mouth. As they grow and their status in the pack's hierarchy becomes clearer, the subordinate wolves continue the pup-like behavior around the more-dominant pack members as a way of keeping everyone happy.

Likewise, when a new adult wolf from the outside seeks permission to join the pack, he assumes submissive postures—crouching, avoiding eye contact, rolling on his back—to let the others know that he's no threat. If he acts submissive in a convincing-enough way, he might be granted membership, and at the very least won't be attacked.

The ultimate submissive gesture among wolves and dogs is seeing a man about a horse. In the wild, if a subordinate wolf sees a man about a horse in the presence of a dominant wolf, it's his way of saying, "Go ahead and kill me. I'm so low compared to you, I won't even fight back," and usually it's enough to avoid any conflict.

But while it's important to understand what a submissive dog says with his actions, it's even more important to know what a dominant pack member says with his. Those in the upper echelons of a pack stare directly at those lower in rank and emit low growls, stand over them, and place paws across their backs.

So guess how your shy dog interprets your attempts to be friendly:

Your Action: loving gaze
His Interpretation: direct stare

Your Action: kissing baby noises
His Interpretation: low growl

Your Action: bending down and reaching toward him
His Interpretation: standing over

Your Action: petting him as he crouches
His Interpretation: paw over the back

Your Action: sliding food under the bed
His Interpretation: the bogeyman is also a vending machine

He's so scared by this point that he'll see a man about a horse on the floor as a final plea for his life. Imagine a giant predatory spider towering twelve feet above you, making weird hissing noises, and extending a hairy arm in your direction; would you lose it or what? That's the level of fear an overly submissive dog experiences every time a human being coos sweet nothings and tries to pet him. When I rescue these types of dogs, I wear sunglasses, squat sideways, and speak in a monotone voice, reciting the ABCs.

Usually, however, we make things even worse for the poor guy, because while we try harder and harder to get him to like us, he becomes more and more afraid. Then, when we scold him for seeing a man about a horse on the floor, he has no other way to tell us how sorry he is for not communicating his intentions more clearly, and so he you-know-whats some more.

In a dog's world, people are his pack members, and if he's yelled at or punished when he's young, or if he doesn't socialize with humans during the first eight weeks of life when he's developing his sense of self, then he will be prone to an inferiority complex that will haunt him throughout his life. Whether you've rescued a shy dog from a pound, a puppy mill, a pet store, or the streets, the answer is not to overwhelm him with love and affection, but rather, to do just the opposite and leave him alone for a while. Ignoring is your best training tool in the beginning; simply be a vending machine.

When Bud rooted himself under the bed, for example, I completely ignored him for three whole days. It was important to let him gain confidence at his own pace, because if I'd spent time trying to coax him out, he would have focused so much on his fear of me that he wouldn't have been able to see the following:

- Me feeding the other dogs.
- Me playing with the other dogs.
- The other dogs playing with each other in my presence.
- A pack ruled by a calm, dignified, exceedingly handsome provider (me), whose stellar leadership abilities create an atmosphere of peace and tranquility among the otherwise unruly rabble (them).

In fact, one of the best ways to lure a shy dog away from his fear is to let him watch more-socialized dogs interact with you. At Stray Rescue, we try to place a feral or overly submissive dog in a foster home where there are other dogs to set an example, because it is *the* best way to show them how the other half lives. Nobody likes to miss out on the fun, so ham it up with your other dogs as if you're throwing a party just to make your neighbors jealous. Jealousy can be a great tool with the shy dog.

During those first three days of Bud's introduction to our pack, I never once bent down and looked at him under the bed. Direct eye contact for any extended period of time is one dog's way of saying to another, "I'm about to kick your ass," so when I changed his water or slid him food, I didn't look sideways at him for a second.

The first big break came when I brought out the hot dogs. As I've explained in other chapters, no dog can resist offal-stuffed intestines, so I sat on the floor near the bed, doled out wiener bits to the other dogs, and, using a magazine as a fan, I waited for the smell to reach Bud. In less than two seconds, his nose went into high gear, his ears picked up, and his eyes darted from one dog to the other as they downed the goods. He knew the party had started without him.

Without making a big scene, I casually tossed a hot-dog slice his way, which he inhaled, and then I continued feeding the others. I didn't immediately toss him a second piece but let him watch the others swarm around me for theirs, and when I heard him whine, I glanced his way for the first time. Then I tossed him his second piece. As anyone addicted to junk food knows, one or two bites just ain't enough, and within seconds, Bud had slunk out from under the bed with just his head peering out, like a Pez candy dispenser waiting for more.

That night when I came home from the shelter, Bud moved his headquarters from under the bed to under my kitchen table, closer to the fridge—the ultimate vending machine—so I locked the other dogs out of the kitchen, sat on top of the table, and tossed hot-dog pieces down onto the floor. With each piece, Bud's nose appeared first, followed by his head, followed by his tongue, which darted out with the agility of an octopus tentacle, grabbed the hot dog piece, and retracted. Then his head disappeared back under the table.

Over the next hour, I tossed the hot dogs farther and farther out, until Bud's entire body emerged from under the table, and by midnight, he stood at the other end of the room catching the treats in his mouth mid-flight as I flung them. Then he threw up because he'd eaten so many hot dogs, and when I inadvertently wailed "NOOOOO," and gagged in too dramatic a fashion, he slunk back under the table, peeing the whole way.

(*Note to Reader*: Because I have avoidance issues, it often takes me days to deal with a pile of dog throw-up. For those of you with similar issues, drop an old towel over the throw-up so you don't have to look at it, and let it sit there for three days, spraying Febreze on it. By that time, it will have hardened up just enough for you to grab it under the towel in one piece, and you can toss both into the outside garbage can in one fell swoop without retching.)

(Note #2 to Reader: If you want to be smart about it, drop your significant other's favorite shirt over the pile. When they ask why it's on the floor, shrug and leave the room. From that point on, it's *their* responsibility.)

Back to Bud. Up until the point when he threw up, I was desensitizing him to his new environment, which meant every time I threw a hot dog farther out and he crawled farther out into the room to get it, he received a reward for braving the unknown. Unfortunately, when I wailed and gagged, it scared him back under the table, so for the next several nights we went through the same exercise, but this time, I wailed "NOOOOO" and gagged each time I threw the hot dog out, so he came to associate me wailing and gagging with receiving a groovy treat.

Likewise, all shy dogs must learn to associate pleasure with what scares them (this is why I smoke, for I use the same technique). Many, for example, see a man about a horse when a person walks in the front door. They do this because when the person walks in, they usually act "aggressively" by bending down (standing over), making weird kissing noises (low growls), and petting them on the head (paw over back).

Again, it's a matter of misinterpretation, so instead of "aggressively" greeting your shy dog at the door, try ignoring him instead. When you first walk in, don't look at him and don't direct any words his way. Then wait for *him* to approach *you*, and when he does, bend down to his level, avoid prolonged eye contact, speak softly without making coochy-coochy-bla-bla-coo baby noises, and pet him under the chin or on the chest between his front legs.

If after a few days of this your shy dog still sees a man about a horse when you arrive, add a little treat every time you walk in the door, but don't just hand it to him—toss it across the room so he has to go and find it. This diverts his focus from fear to food, and if you're consistent, he'll soon associate your arrival with hunting for treats and forget he was ever afraid.

Whatever you do, don't yell or scold him if he sees a man about a horse in front of you. It's tempting, I know, and this is where it gets tough, because no matter what you do to assure him of your affection, he still acts like you're going to kill him. It's easy to lose your temper, but if you do, it will only make him more scared and confused, and he'll see more men about more horses even more often.

(*Cleanup Tip*: Buy the cheapest diapers available rather than paper towels; they absorb the pee quicker and better, and if you are single like me, the grocery-store clerk thinks you're just an economical dad who buys way too many douches (see chapter 1) and diapers.)

Finally, always let him win. When you play tug-of-war, let him win. When you wrestle on the floor, let him win. When he paws you for attention, let him win. Build his confidence up one win at a time, and in the end, which is just a few short months away, you'll see a much less submissive dog.

As for Bud . . . Fortunately, we found a family to adopt him. Unfortunately, it took a long time, I guess because of the following description we put under his picture on our Web site:

Oh, by the way, that family is *me*. Bud is pretty normal now, sleeps *on* the bed and not under it, loves playing with toys, and loves to be petted, but to this day, he eats his meals under the bed. I find that endearing, for it's a constant reminder to me that nobody, whether two-legged or four-, is perfect.

« Bud's a little shy, so he should have a family with other dogs and parents willing to let him win tug-of-war games and yell "NOOOOO" and then make gagging noises in a convincing way whenever something scares him . . .

CHAPTER THIRTEEN

I Love Old Dogs

Dear Randy,

   We adopted a dog from you several years ago. Back then she was an adorable puppy with cute little freckles on her nose. Her name was Cuddles, but we renamed her Casey. She's a wonderful dog who gets along great with the other dogs in the neighborhood and is completely housebroken. She also graduated at the top of her obedience class.

   The reason I am writing to you is that I'm afraid we're going to have to return Casey to your organization. She is getting old. She's about ten now and her hair is turning gray around her muzzle, and we no longer see her freckles. Her teeth are showing signs of tartar and her eyes are getting cloudy. I understand this comes with old age, but recently she knocked over the trash can and is still afraid of storms after all these years. Please let me know what I have to do to bring her back. Also, would it be possible to get another puppy after we return her?

   Please contact us as soon as possible.

   Darren and Dodo Dump

```
Dear Darren and Dodo,
    If you didn't want a dog, why did
you get a puppy in the first place?
    Yours truly,
    Randy Grim
```

his one had me shaking like a rattle in the hands of
a psychotic baby. I was pissed, and thought it had to
be a joke. How could this be for real? So, I did what
any good Rescue Randy would do and called to talk with the
Dumps, live and in-person. It went something like this:

Randy: Umm . . . Hi, it's Randy from Stray Rescue. I
got your e-mail. I just want to make sure . . . umm . . .
is this for real?

The Dumps: Why would you think it's not?

Randy: Umm . . . because, basically, you just seem to
be tired of Casey, and umm . . . I see no real reason
for you to return her. (I knew this would probably
tick off the Dumps, and it did.)

The Dumps: How dare you judge us! We have the
right to keep her or get rid of her without any crap
from you!

Randy: Okay, okay, calm down. Just drop her off,
please, you stupid-ass morons.

No, I really didn't say exactly that. The "stupid-ass morons" part came out of my mouth after I'd hung up.

Let's look more closely at this letter. The first sentence states that they adopted her several years ago as a puppy, but now she is ten. Did Casey get some sort of accelerated aging disease, or is there something fishy with their story (because it stinks)? Doesn't the word *several* mean something like three? So the Dumps are dissembling. Several years is not ten years old, except maybe in giant tortoise years.

Show of hands—how many of you reading this book right now would want a dog that had these characteristics? She's a wonderful dog. She gets along great with the other dogs in the neighborhood, and is completely housebroken. She also graduated at the top of her obedience class. My hunch is that many of you are clutching this book in one hand as if it were the doggie bible and raising the other to the sky, shouting "Hallelujah!" If you are like me, none of my kids (kids=dogs) are as well-rounded as Casey. In fact, most of mine ride the short yellow bus.

Another show of hands: How many of you stopped loving or caring for your parents just because the inevitable happened, and they got old? (You all better *not* be holding up those hands.)

I pray that dog karma exists. When the Dumps get old and gray and lose those cute freckles and their teeth, develop cloudy eyes, and accidentally knock over their own adult Depends diaper pail, I hope they get sent away to the nursing home from hell. The one with Nurse Ratched, who forces you to eat Jell-O while playing Hell's version of a never-ending bingo game where there is never a winner—only losers with cloudy cataracts.

I love old dogs.

Casey was getting the ax, but what was also very disconcerting to me was the Dumps' desire to have a new puppy. Do they think dogs are like cars, where you can just trade in the older model (before it dies) for something younger? If they'd written because they wanted to adopt a new puppy to help keep Casey feeling young and to give her some company, that would have been great. But that wasn't the case at all. I feel awful knowing they've probably adopted a new puppy from somewhere else by now. If it's not the perfect puppy, what will they do next? Let's just hope the new puppy dumps on the Dumps and destroys their home. Heck, I hope the puppy throws in a bite or two for good measure, and then runs away and lives with someone like sweet little Jimmy from *Lassie Come Home*.

How would I solve the problem so they would keep Casey? My advice would be intense daily therapy with the world's leading psychiatrists, and if that didn't work, try Dr. Phil. If he can't straighten them out, God help us all—especially if you bark.

Darren and Dodo, I take solace in hoping Nurse Ratched and her never-ending supply of lime Jell-O will be waiting for them in their glory years. Fortunately, Casey found a new home with new parents who are over sixty years of age, and who understand where Casey is on her journey through life.

I love old dogs.

Enjoy Your Senior Dog

- Exercise! He still loves his walks. The smells of the outdoors, peeing over another dog's pee and sniffing a good butt or two is the spice of life for elderly pooches. Walking helps keep the aged bones strong.
- A warm, soft, cozy bed for achy joints. Add a pillow for his snoozing head. Horsey likes a 300 thread count like his dad.
- Invest in a baby gate to prevent stair falls. Easy simple solution. I use it on my mom, too.
- Oh, my wonderful ramp! Use it for your bed, car, or even bathtub.
- Elderly dogs should see the doc twice a year for wellness exams.
- A senior diet keeps him healthy, not portly.

CHAPTER FOURTEEN

To Crate or Not to Crate

Dear Randy,

    I adopted Fred from you about six months ago, but I'm afraid it's not a good match. Every time I leave the house, Fred gets in the garbage and chews up throw pillows, dirty laundry, shoes—you name it; he destroys it. I don't believe in using a crate, that's like a prison for a dog. He is about eight months old now. I'm at my wit's end and think maybe I need a different dog—maybe an older one?

    Thanks,

    Obstinate Ollie

Dear Ollie,

    Try using your noodle. Think Ollie, think!

    Sincerely,

    Randy Grim

While you and I may not like the thought of being in crates (although I welcome the thought when I read some of these letters), a dog's point of view is very different: they *like* being in crates.

Consider the wolves. For them, a den is a place where the pups spend their first few weeks of life with their mother. It's not shared with the rest of the pack and is a warm, safe place where they sleep, eat, and play. Wolves make their dens by digging with their paws, which is a trait passed on to my own crew and which is why my backyard looks like the moon's surface.

So don't think of a crate as a prison cell. It's a dog's version of a den, and if you have problems with the idea of crate training your dog, think of it instead as den training.

But a crate is much more than a den, it provides a secure nesting space free from all other distractions. It is your dog's haven and your ticket to sanity. A comfy den should not be kept in too bright or busy of a room, because it's supposed to be a place for the dog to decompress, his own private Idaho where he can be alone, kick back and play with his toys or chew on his bones in privacy.

The point is that crating a dog is not cruel as long as you don't turn the crate into a tool of punishment. It should *never* be used as such. Think about it: when did having to go to our rooms as children for punishment ever work? I still snuck out the window and pulled off my shenanigans. Dogs are no different, so let's do this exercise mantra aloud, before we go any further:

ALL DOGS LOVE SHENANIGANS

ALL DOGS LOVE SHENANIGANS

ALL DOGS LOVE SHENANIGANS

Repeat this fifty times so it sinks in. Shenanigans=Dogs. Do you think your dog will play with his X-Box, listen to music and vacuum while you are gone? Playing in the garbage *is* your dog's X-Box.

Basically, I divide my life into two parts: before the crate and after the crate. Before the crate, Steffi and Patsy (whom I call my little lesbians, because they are inseparable) played Shenanigans whenever I turned my back on them. Those two dogs tag teamed attacks on my couch, my bed, and my closet the *second* I stopped paying attention. I even had them professionally trained but all that accomplished was a perfect "sit" next to whatever they just destroyed.

Then one night during the Christmas holidays, I got a call from Jenn that one of the dogs in the shelter was going into labor. She was a ghetto yellow Labrador mix rescue who was malnourished, suffering from heartworm and had no real nipples for the pups to nurse on, so I knew Jenn's call was an emergency. Instead of locking Steffi and Patsy into the kitchen as I normally did, I just turned on the radio loud and bolted out the door thinking, "How much damage could they really do?"

During the course of the next several hours, as the mom dog labored in vain, the radio at the shelter—set to the same station as the one I left on at my house—played the same series of Christmas songs over and over and over. For some reason, . . . *here comes Suzy Snowflake dressed in her snow-white gown* . . . got so stuck in my head, it was if my brain's cerebellum bled the words. . . . *Dressed in her snow-white gown, weee the ride's on me* . . .

Eventually we took Suzy (as we ended up naming her) to the vet where an emergency C-section was performed. She lived, some pups died and I was delirious from lack of sleep. All I could think about as I approached my house still humming the song was crawling into bed and sleeping for the next twenty-four hours straight.

When I opened the door, well . . . picture the most evil hooligans armed with machetes declaring war on your stuff: overturned garbage in every room; sheets ripped completely off the beds; there were actually pictures from the wall on the floor. As I wondered around in a daze, the radio I left on for the dogs played . . . *Here comes Suzy Snowflake dressed in her snow-white gown* . . . *weeee* . . . like the background music of a movie not far flung from *The Shining*. That awful song must have had something to do with my destroyed home.

Upstairs, my mattress sported a colossal hole in it as if a meteor ripped through my ceiling and into my bed. Bits and pieces of my shirts, shoes, and books littered the floor. I eventually found Steffi and Patsy on the stripped guest bed engulfed in clouds of pillow stuffing. When they heard me gasp, their faces popped up out of the white stuffing, they cocked their heads sideways in opposite directions, and then promptly did skilled "sits" next to all the mess they made.

Defeated, I climbed into bed fully dressed with my butt fitting snugly into the newly formed crater that once was my mattress and hummed myself to sleep, *dressed in her snow-white gown . . . weeee . . .*

That's when I purchased two more crates.

Wire crates work best and allow a panoramic view for the pooch. Your dog's crate should be just large enough for him to stand up and turn around in. If your dog is still growing, choose a crate size that will accommodate his adult size. Block off the excess crate space so your dog can't eliminate at one end and retreat to the other. Place it in an area of the house he enjoys hanging out in. Mine are in my bedroom next to the crater bed and TV.

Desensitizing your dog to her new den will be the first step. Start by keeping the front door off the crate for easy access, and line the crate with comfortable bedding such as fleece. Let her spend a day just looking and sniffing her new digs. Once she sees that it doesn't transform into a metallic canine-eating monster, start putting her favorite treats and toys inside the den. Use gentle praise, and don't make a big fuss about it. Let her instincts start to kick in.

If she is being stubborn about it or shows no interest, try feeding her meals in the crate. We all like eating in bed.

After she waltzes in and out on her own and believes she has some cool new pad, it is time for tough love. Feed her in the crate but this time close the door. Pretend it is no big deal and walk away out of sight but stay close enough to hear what will probably come next, whining. Do *not* open that door. Go grab an adult beverage and sip it until the whining stops. Once she simmers down, release the door, and again, don't make a fuss about it.

The first time you leave her alone in her crate for any length of time, grab an old dirty shirt out of the hamper with your magnificent stench intact and toss it in her den. Your smells will help her later on feel more comfortable knowing you are still close by somewhere. Now go grab a leash or a ball and get her tired, because you want a pooped pooch. Snatch a Kong toy, available at any pet store, and stuff it with peanut butter or cheese. Place the Kong in the crate with her. Now, shut the door. She will probably howl, so turn up the TV or buy earplugs for you and your neighbors.

In time and especially with food, your dog will cease howling or whining. In fact many dogs pick up on their guardian's actions and will boogie to their den when they see you grab your keys, for it all starts to become routine, habitual. My lovely old pit-hound mix Hannah is always in her den when she hears the shower going. She knows a clean Dad means he is about to leave the house. Hannah doesn't need to be crated anymore. Her shenanigans stopped many years ago but she still goes to her crate with her favorite toy every time I leave. I don't even shut the crate door. The lesbians, however, get locked in for maximum security.

Crating should never be used for punishment or endless hours of confinement. We all love going to bed but we do want to wake up and go to the bathroom eventually. This is a den, a home within a home. Make it nice.

My old chow Bear knows how to properly use a crate. He actually enjoys hanging out in one even though he has never been crated. Why train a perfectly behaved dog to use the crate, you might ask . . . one word: K-A-T-R-I-N-A.

After rescuing so many dogs during hurricanes Katrina and Gustav and seeing so many dogs die or left behind because the guardians couldn't or wouldn't use a crate, I go nuts. We live in a world where natural and unnatural disasters can happen on a dime. Your pooch will thank you for having a safe den to nest in while you ride out the catastrophe. Hotels, emergency shelters and more importantly your family will be more open to take you and the dog in if you have a crate in tow. Like a good scout, be prepared.

Den dos and don'ts

- Do use your crate for housebreaking
- Do use your crate if you have a destructive dog
- Do make sure it is a fun, cozy, secure place with treats and toys
- Do feed your dog in the crate
- Don't replace the crate as a socialization tool
- Don't use as a remedy for separation anxiety, for your dog could get hurt
- Don't use a crate for punishment
- Don't crate for more than eight hours with an adult dog; much less with puppies
- Don't listen to a song called "Suzy Snowflake"

Alternatives to crating can be even more stimulating and effective for your dog. Hire a pet walker while you are gone or use a doggy day care. Doggy day care is all the rage and you bring home a very social pup. We put our human kids in day care so why not the dog? I prefer this over long hours of crating.

As for Ollie, his sanity has returned and Fred now uses a crate and calls it his den. His new throw pillows lay beautifully on his couch in one piece and the garbage now stays in the can. Shenanigans are now supervised, the way it should have been from the get go. Fred didn't get dumped.

Remember a crate isn't cruel unless you make it that way. Don't screw up.

CHAPTER FIFTEEN

Affordable Strays

Dear Randy,
        We found a stray dog several months
ago and didn't know what to do with her,
so we kept her. We've fallen absolutely
in love with her, but my husband has
lost his job, and now we don't know if
we can afford to keep her any more.
        Thanks for any advice!

I received this not long ago, and my heart went out to these folks. It's always tough when you find a stray dog, and the decision of whether or not to rescue her isn't made any easier during hard economic times. So here's my two cents' worth on both subjects . . .

In terms of what to do if you find a stray dog, remember that your local shelter is already bursting at the seams, and always full. Most cities and towns have a very high kill rate at their shelters, and chances of a stray making it out alive can be slim at best. Skip the shelters. First, keep the pooch safe and secure in your home, in a crate or a spare room. I have used my bathroom plenty of times, and I've finally gotten used to being stared at as I drop the kids off at the pool.

Kindness is key: Treat the dog as if it were your own, but keep him separated from your other pets until you've had a chance to take him to the veterinarian. At the vet's you can have him scanned for a microchip, which could solve everything. If your luck is like mine, though, there probably won't be a microchip. Have the vet give him his basic shots and exam, but tell the doc that he is a stray and maybe he'll go easy on the price.

Find a Stray Dog's Guardians

- Place a found-dog ad in the local paper; these ads are usually free. Provide a generic description so when people call, you can ask for a more detailed description of Fido. This helps keep the crazies away, like the creeps who sell animals to laboratories.
- Make flyers and post them near the area he was found and at area animal-ish types of places, such as groomers, pet stores, etc.

- Surf the Net and post on craigslist.com and on lostandfound.com.

If you still haven't found Fido's guardians and it's five days (and two bottles of vodka) later, maybe by now the li'l guy has started to grow on you, and you decide to adopt the dog yourself. You just won the Randy Grim Merit Award.

If you throw my merit award in the trash and don't want to keep Fido, then place him yourself. You can do it. Feel free to go to www.strayrescue.org and use our online adoption form. Pretend you are a shelter. Be picky.

Finding a suitable home takes some time, but it helps to network with friends, family, and coworkers. Never place an ad saying "free to a good home," or the crazies will come a-knocking. Charge the same adoption fee as your local shelter, and in return, the new guardian will get a dog that is vaccinated, microchipped, de-sexed, and given a clean bill of health. You can now go back to the trash can, pull out your crumpled-up Merit Award, and enjoy a martini, for you just made the world a better place.

If you do decide to keep the dog or if you already have a dog but have fallen on hard times, there is a solution, at least with my organization, and I'll bet many others.

If you're giving up on your dog because you can't afford his food and basic care, here are some money-saving tips:

- To save money on food, buy in bulk when on sale. Discount and club stores offer less-expensive products than your grocery store, and dollar stores are now carrying higher-quality brands of dog food, too.

- Be a smart shopper; shop around, and use your coupons. If you're shopping on-line, search for coupon codes and you can save a lot.

- Purchase pet health insurance, usually about $20 a month. Many dog insurance policies also cover wellness exams, including the dog's vaccinations, heartworm tests and meds, fecal tests, and more. You would get what you invested back within a year. Be responsible and make sure your dog sees the vet annually. Wellness exams can prevent something much worse later on. If an unexpected injury or illness occurs, you are covered, and you'll be kissing your insurance bill for saving your butt.

  A) If it is a surgery you can't afford, ask a rescue group or shelter if they can help; in return, you can step up to the plate and volunteer and/or foster as a way of paying back the debt.

B) Ask to set up a payment plan with your local veterinarian.

- Most cities offer assistance programs that spay and neuter for free, or for next to nothing.

Afterword: Randy on a Soapbox

The excuses you've read in this book are real; the names have been changed to protect the guilty.

Often I am asked, "How do you handle the sadness of rescue and returned dogs?" I usually say, "With vodka and Xanax," which is my way of staying sane and avoiding sucker-punching the next person who walks in the shelter and says, "I can't keep my dog because . . ."

For over a decade, I have been given every excuse imaginable about why I must take their dog off their hands. The time has come for me to wire my jaws shut from this nauseating meal and to teach people the proper way to care for their dog—a much healthier diet.

Many lame, eye-rolling excuses as well as outright lies are given when someone forces us to take their "beloved" pet, or when families come back and say they need to return the pet they adopted from Stray Rescue. In my experience, about 2 percent of the excuses are understandable to my psyche. It's the remaining 98 percent that causes everyone at the shelter to experience flu-like symptoms, or to have to fight the urge to go "postal," and/or break out the booze.

I have endured many uncomfortable close encounters with "dumpers," my term for these folks. Once the leash is out of their hands, the dumper always scurries out the door like a rodent on a mission for a piece of cheese, seemingly guilt-free and ready to start their new life, companion-animal-free. Left on their own, their former faithful friend now has to adjust to an anxiety-filled life behind bars, a pooch prison, waiting for her third lease on life. Grrrrrr. I hope the dumper's cheese is spoiled.

There are hundreds of reasons why companion animals are turned in to our nation's strained shelter system. Most shelters have heard every excuse known to man and dog. The most oft-used reasons range from "We're moving" or "We're having a baby" to "My dog is boring" and the ever-common "We don't want to put up a fence." (In actuality we did have a dog returned for being lazy. I guess it was my fault; I should have given the dumpers some "doggie uppers" when they adopted.)

The problem starts where problems usually do—at the beginning. Shelter staffs are not trained to provide pet guardians with proper information about training a new dog or puppy, the importance of spaying and neutering their pet, nor solutions to behavioral problems, should they arise after adoption. Likewise, new guardians are not instructed on how to choose the proper dog for their family and lifestyle. Nor do they put much thought into the "purchase" of a new *life*, a new member of the family.

Dogs are often chosen because they are a particular breed—one that's recently been featured in a popular movie, TV show, or commercial, like a current trendy hairstyle. Another high priority is the color of the dog. If you are a black dog— uh-oh . . . your chances of adoption are pretty low. Rarely do prospective adoptive families look for personality traits that are a good match for them, or think about what level of energy is best suited for their lifestyle. Hordes of perfect companions with the most loving and loyal personalities are passed over in favor of those with a high "cuteness" quotient—you know, the Benji factor. Just as beauty in humans is more valued in our society than a great personality and a generous heart, the funny-looking dog, the all-black one, and those with the not-so-perfect bodies (like most of us two-legged beings) are doomed most of the time. I think the voluminous number of those "make me perfect" reality television shows contribute to the problem. It drives me nutty to know that all of this unconditional love is euthanized so effortlessly and with such lack of blame.

Our twenty-first century society increasingly expects all relevant information to be simply handed to us. Maybe we don't stop to consider what we know versus what we don't know about our companion animals. Maybe we think we have the innate intelligence to guide us in raising our kids and our dogs. Consequently, when our new pet gets too big, is too energetic, or isn't playful enough, it's not our fault. The problem must lie with the pet, so off he goes to the nearest animal shelter. Since most pets are delivered to "humane" shelters, our guilt is somewhat alleviated; after all, it wasn't *our* fault. It was entirely Fido's doing. As long as we avoid learning the statistics of how many animals actually make it out of the shelters (only a small percentage get adopted), we can live with the "humane" fantasy we've created in order to cope with the reality.

There is a good chance that many of us will "try" again, bringing home another dog, hoping that this time our new pet will be as perfect as the ones from the commercials and the Westminster Dog Show. Unless we take the time to learn patience, along with the basics of dog behavior, and unless we're willing to give our new companion plenty of time and attention, chances are that our poorly chosen pet will experience a short life.

Research has shown that most animals are relinquished to a shelter because of behavioral issues, which are caused by a variety of contributing factors. One colossal reason is the mass production of puppies in commercial kennels (puppy mills) and the lack of responsible breeding practices by backyard breeders, which lead to numerous health and behavioral issues that many guardians with varying degrees of commitment can't or won't handle.

Animals bred and raised in puppy mills are subject to every disease known to man and dog. They are often kept in cramped cages all their young lives without any contact with humans or other dogs, which in turn can do a number on the canine psyche. Their unsuspecting new families often find themselves with a dog who is terrified of open spaces, is incapable of being house-trained in a timely fashion, and who, bewildered by the gigantic humans around him, reacts by being aggressive or by peeing on the floor at the sight of anything over two feet tall. Solution: off to the pound, the dumping ground.

Most people don't realize what constitutes a puppy mill. In actuality, the term "canine concentration camp" would be more apt. Breeding adult dogs are not given adequate housing, food, exercise, or attention, and usually, little to no medical care. Consequently, they are experiencing hunger, pain, and illness on a daily basis, which naturally causes aggression. Most are unable to properly care for their puppies because their own health is so compromised. Puppies are often weaned away from their mothers and separated from their siblings way too early when sold to brokers. These intermediaries care for the puppies until they are sold to a pet store. This lack of bonding with their mothers and siblings causes many socialization issues that affect the dog (and their adoptive family) later in life.

Plenty of research has shown that this inadequate socialization at a young age leads to a high incidence of dominance-type aggression, as well as fear/defensive aggression. Consequently, these puppy-mill dogs are genetically inferior, both physically and emotionally. Research has also shown that more than fifty genetic diseases can predispose an animal toward aggression/behavioral issues.

Other causes of behavioral issues not related to puppy-mill breeding include chaining or tethering animals for long periods of time, and extended periods of isolation. Animals feel secure when they are part of a pack, and being left alone for twelve hours a day while their "family" pack is at work (and happy hour) is very stressful to companion animals. Likewise, reinforcing unwanted behaviors with attention or inducing fear through violence and threatening mannerisms can result in a dog behaving poorly. Lack of exercise and mental stimulation can also lead to destructive behaviors, as animals have a great deal of energy that needs to be expended daily. (This sounds almost human, doesn't it?)

Only 12 to 14 percent of dogs are adopted from shelters nationally. The average age of an animal that enters a shelter is between six and eighteen months. Approximately 85 percent of those "in the market" for a pet desire a dog younger than one year old. Older dogs have virtually no chance for adoption; their stay in the shelter is usually a brief interlude before death. Even though the senior dogs are usually the easiest to deal with, they don't have much hope, as youth usually wins out. The stigma attached to shelter animals is that they are "used goods" and must somehow be defective. It certainly doesn't help that most are mixed breeds, although purebreds do make up one-quarter of the nation's shelter population.

More than 27,000 animals are destroyed every day; more than 1,000 are destroyed every hour; and one animal is destroyed every minute of every hour of every day. A very alarming statistic.

Let's not forget that we are dealing with a *life* here—a new family member who has emotional needs, who feels most secure when part of a "family" pack, and who experiences an array of emotions ranging from pain and loss to joy and depression. As a society, don't we all consider ourselves highly evolved human beings who respect life, have strong family values, try to feed the hungry and aid the suffering of those less fortunate? The only difference between humans and animals is our native language. Humans and dogs have all the same body parts and functions, along with intelligence and feelings. Experts feel that our four-legged family member is basically the same as a four-year-old child (which I always saw as a plus, but I must be in the minority). Their ability to learn is about the same; they love life and get very energized when good things happen; they eat with gusto, love to be cuddled, and to play and play and play. Although many animal guardians "get it," way too many don't. Why is that?

Many good, hardworking people often inherit the mentality that the family dog is basically disposable property—a common trait passed down unconsciously. It's time for these people to wake up and smell the Milk-Bones.

I could have made this book merely a bitching session, but my bona fide reason to write this book is to give potential "dumpers" a chance at redemption—an opportunity to deal with and solve the problems of their companion animal before burdening their local shelter, already bursting at the seams. It is also a book for us "normal" guardians with problem pooches.

Between us, my hope is that you won't give up on the one true loyal being in your life, the family dog. You know, man's best friend? And hopefully, you will be "trained" to do right by your companion animal and will not end up in my next book.